Blue & Gray Magazine's

HISTORY AND TOUR GUIDE

OF THE

BATTLE OF
FIVE FORKS

by Chris Calkins

Historian, Petersburg National Battlefield, Virginia

Including the Battles of Lewis' Farm, White Oak Road, and Dinwiddie Court House, With Supplemental Tours of the Battle of Hatcher's Run and the Fight at Namozine Church

To obtain information on other titles or special arrangements offered by The General's Books and *Blue & Gray Magazine*, write to the address above, or contact us by phone: 614-870-1861; fax: 614-870-7881; email: bgeditors@aol.com; or through our website: www.bluegraymagazine.com.

This book includes material previously published in *Blue & Gray Magazine*: Vol. VII, Issue 6, August 1990; and Vol. IX, Issue 4, April 1992.

ISBN 1-891515-07-1

TABLE OF CONTENTS

THE General's TOUR™

Including the Battles of Lewis' Farm, White Oak Road, and Dinwiddie Court House, With Supplemental Tours of the Battle of Hatcher's Run and the Fight at Namozine Church

PERIOD PHOTOGRAPHS

MODERN PHOTOGRAPHS

MAPS

NOTE ABOUT MAPS

The Battle and Campaign Maps in this book are consistent in presentation as to relative size of units. The symbols (below left), which appear on the maps with the name of the commander, indicate unit organization. Refer also to the Orders of Battle on Pp. 169 and 175.

★ / ☆	Infantry / Cavalry Brigade
★★ / ☆☆	Infantry / Cavalry Division
★★★ / ☆☆☆	Infantry / Cavalry Corps
★★★★	Army

Ulysses S. Grant, USA

THE BATTLE OF HATCHER'S RUN

To Cut the Remaining Supply Lines

February 5-7, 1865

by Chris Calkins

Historian, Petersburg National Battlefield, Virginia

Maps prepared by Dave Roth of
Blue & Gray Magazine

Refer to the Tour Maps on Pp. 136-137 & 165.

ALTHOUGH THE MILITARY OPERATIONS around Petersburg were geographically much farther south in Virginia than those in the previous three years, the winter of 1864-65 was remembered by the soldiers as "one of unusual severity." In a raid from Petersburg to Belfield/Hicksford (now Emporia, near the North Carolina border) by the Union Army in early December, the soldiers experienced freezing rain and snow flurries on the march. On New Year's Day it snowed, with an accumulation of a few inches, then throughout January the men in the trenches saw scattered snow, rain and sleet, with generally frosty weather.

Normally the armies would not make any major military movements during the dead of winter, having learned from their mistakes earlier in the war. Union General Ambrose E. Burnside's infamous "Mud March" of January 1863, was a perfect example. Ulysses S. Grant, on the other hand, wanted to keep up his relentless pressure on Robert E. Lee's forces around Petersburg, the "Cockade City," and the threats of bad weather and muddy roads were not about to stop him.

In early 1865 the Federal army's two main strategic objectives along the Petersburg front were: the Boydton Plank Road, an intermediate wagon supply route to the city; and the South Side Railroad, a major supply artery from Lynchburg and the Shenandoah Valley. If both of these could be eliminated, the siege operations could be lifted and Lee would be forced to abandon Petersburg and possibly Richmond.

Robert E. Lee, CSA

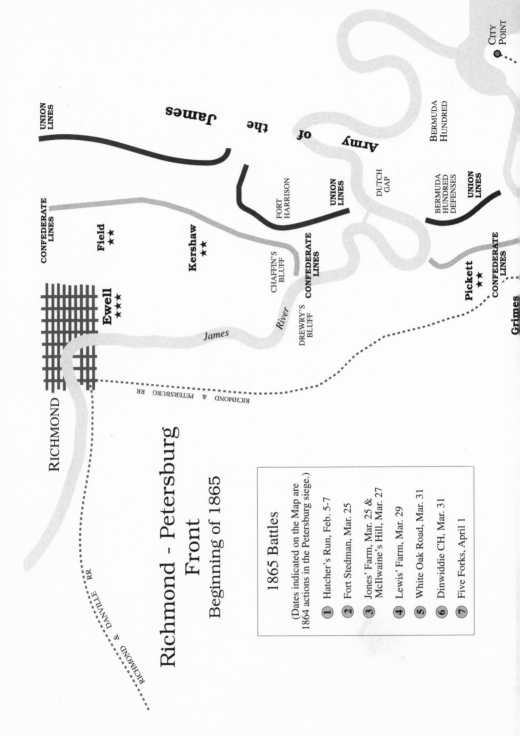

CITY POINT

UNION LINES

James

the

of

Army

BERMUDA HUNDRED

CONFEDERATE LINES

Field ★★

Kershaw ★★

FORT HARRISON

UNION LINES

DUTCH GAP

BERMUDA HUNDRED DEFENSES

UNION LINES

Ewell ★★★

CHAFFIN'S BLUFF

CONFEDERATE LINES

Pickett ★★

CONFEDERATE LINES

RICHMOND

River

DREWRY'S BLUFF

Grimes

James

RICHMOND & PETERSBURG RR

RICHMOND & DANVILLE RR

Richmond - Petersburg Front
Beginning of 1865

1865 Battles

(Dates indicated on the Map are 1864 actions in the Petersburg siege.)

1. Hatcher's Run, Feb. 5-7
2. Fort Stedman, Mar. 25
3. Jones' Farm, Mar. 25 & McIlwaine's Hill, Mar. 27
4. Lewis' Farm, Mar. 29
5. White Oak Road, Mar. 31
6. Dinwiddie CH, Mar. 31
7. Five Forks, April 1

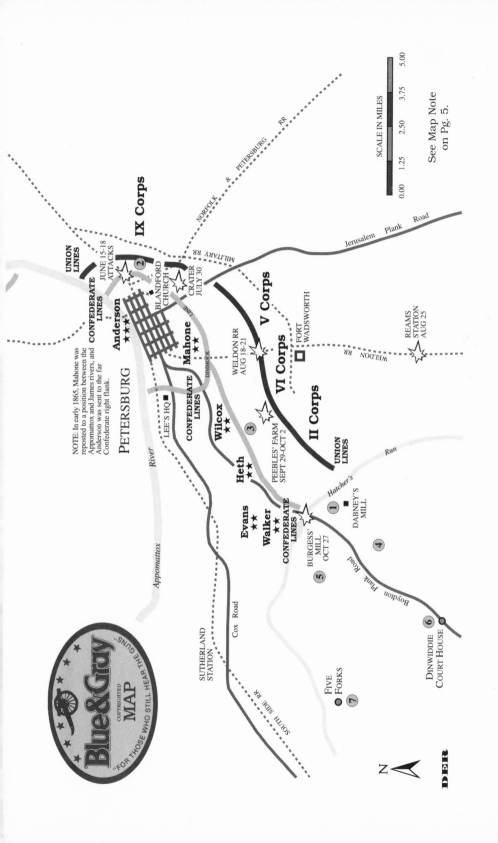

SCALE IN MILES

0.00   1.25   2.50   3.75   5.00

See Map Note
on Pg. 5.

IX Corps

V Corps

VI Corps

II Corps

UNION
LINES

UNION
LINES

CONFEDERATE
LINES

CONFEDERATE
LINES

CONFEDERATE
LINES

JUNE 15-18
ATTACKS

CRATER
JULY 30

BLANDFORD
CHURCH

Anderson ★★★

Mahone ★★

Wilcox ★★

Heth ★★

Evans ★★

Walker ★★

PETERSBURG

LEE'S HQ ■

FORT
WADSWORTH

WELDON RR
AUG 18-21

PEEBLES' FARM
SEPT 29-OCT 2

REAMS
STATION
AUG 25

NOTE: In early 1865, Mahone was
reposted to a position between the
Appomattox and James rivers, and
Anderson was sent to the far
Confederate right flank.

NORFOLK   &   PETERSBURG   RR

Jerusalem   Plank   Road

MILITARY RR

DIMMOCK LINE

WELDON RR

River

Appomattox

Run

Hatcher's

DABNEY'S
MILL

BURGESS'
MILL
OCT 27

Boydton Plank Road

DINWIDDIE
COURT HOUSE

FIVE
FORKS

SUTHERLAND
STATION

Cox   Road

SOUTH SIDE RR

① ② ③ ④ ⑤ ⑥ ⑦

N

DER

Blue&Gray
COPYRIGHTED
MAP
"FOR THOSE WHO STILL HEAR THE GUNS."

With the Weldon Railroad from North Carolina having been cut to Petersburg, forty miles below the city in the area of Belfield/Hicksford, supplies coming up that line had to be unloaded at the latter place, then transported by wagon cross-country up the Meherrin River Valley to the Boydton Plank Road. Upon reaching that turnpike, they passed through Dinwiddie Court House and on to Petersburg. To intercept and break up this supply route, Grant decided to send his one cavalry division, under General David McM. Gregg, to the county seat village of Dinwiddie Court House, supported by two corps of Federal infantry. General Gouverneur K. Warren, with the V Corps, would follow Gregg and cross to the south of Hatcher's Run, taking position along Vaughan Road half-way between the creek and Dinwiddie Court House. General Andrew A. Humphreys, having recently replaced Winfield Scott Hancock in command of the Union II Corps, was to hold positions along Hatcher's Run at the Vaughan Road crossing and at Armstrong's Mill. These troops would guard the movement from the north.

The first couple days in February were somewhat pleasant, although cold and frosty. At 3:00 a.m. on the 5th the march began from the established Federal lines southwest of Petersburg, the men advancing across three or four miles of new territory. A soldier on the march remarked that "the country around is low and swampy, cut up by ravines, and covered with forests traversed here and there by narrow country roads." When eventually in position, Humphreys would begin entrenching within four miles of Warren's corps. Humphreys only took two of his three divisions with him on this movement, under Generals Gershom Mott and Thomas Smyth, and the two units built breastworks through the numerous pine and oak forests and fields making up the Tucker and Armstrong farms.

John B. Gordon, CSA

One brigade, under General P. Regis de Trobriand, forced a crossing to the south of the run and built an arc-shaped line protecting Vaughan Road. Separating the two divisions north of the run was a swamp through which ran a small tributary called Rocky Branch. Small farm roads intersected the area, with only one, Duncan Road, being of any consequence. Completing their breastworks, the Federals faced north, with the main Confederate line guarding the Boydton Plank Road visible about 1,000 yards distant. Between the two lines was the Thompson farm, also made up of scattered woods, fields and Reedy Branch of Arthur Swamp to the east.

General Lee received word of the Federal expedition while at church in Petersburg, and quickly rode out for his lines near Hatcher's Run. In that sector he had General Henry Heth's division (of General A. P. Hill's Third Corps) holding the north side, and it was his trenches that faced Humphreys and protected the plank road. To the west and south of the run past Burgess' Mill was the recently arrived Confederate Second Corps of General John B. Gordon. Reaching the Petersburg front in December from the Shenandoah Valley, Gordon had two divisions with him, under Generals John Pegram and Clement Evans. Camped in reserve along the Boydton Plank Road, and nearer to Petersburg, was General William Mahone's division, now under the temporary command of General Joseph Finegan, Mahone being sick. The only Confederate cavalry available in the area was that of Lee's son, William Henry Fitzhugh Lee, nicknamed "Rooney," and he too was summoned to the area, his camps being almost 40 miles away.

Beginning about 3:45 and lasting past 5:00 p.m., Confederate artillery opened on the Federals from the trenches as two separate Southern infantry battlelines formed to assault the breastworks. General Evans' division was brought up and tried to turn Smyth's

Battle of Hatcher's Run
Feb. 5, 1865

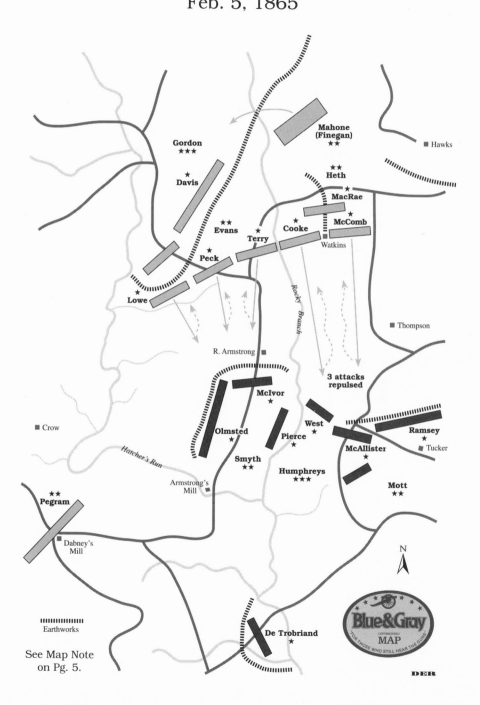

position. At the same time, Heth's Division emerged from the woods on the Thompson farm and made three unsuccessful attacks on Mott, the brunt of which fell upon Colonel Robert McAllister's brigade. Not being able to break the Federal line, the Confederates continued their artillery fire until dark, while the infantry fell back into their entrenchments.

With word of the fighting on the evening of the 5th, General Grant sent reinforcements to Warren and Humphreys, namely the divisions under Generals John Hartranft (IX Corps) and Frank Wheaton (VI Corps) to fall in on Humphreys' right. The Federal cavalry, having reached the Boydton Plank Road that day, captured less than two dozen wagons, and finding little more, were ordered to Vaughan Road with Warren. Orders were now given to push for the South Side Railroad, if possible. That night Colonel Henry Morrow of the V Corps remembered "the night was intensely cold . . . & the men built fires and lay down to get what sleep they might. The troops had moved without tents or blankets & much suffering was the consequence—."

Having crossed to the south of Hatcher's Run on Monday, February 6, about 1:00 p.m. Warren made a reconnaissance with General Samuel Crawford's division, supported by the division of General Romeyn Ayres, on his left, south along Vaughan Road to the intersection with the Dabney's Steam-Sawmill Road. At that point they turned northwest up the lumbermill road and proceeded for about a mile. Simultaneously, Gregg's horsemen moved down Vaughan Road to Gravelly Run to protect Warren's left flank. His remaining division, General Charles Griffin's, was in reserve to cover this movement.

Operating against the Federals in this area, which was criss-crossed by many small farm roads and dotted with forests, were both divisions of General John B. Gordon's Confederate corps. With them was Rooney

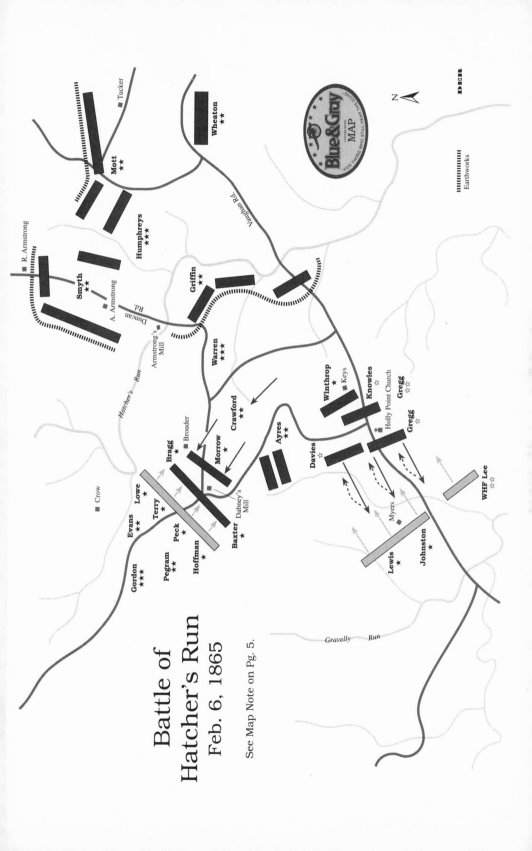

Battle of
Hatcher's Run
Feb. 6, 1865

See Map Note on Pg. 5.

Lee's cavalry division, just arrived from Belfield. Gordon allowed John Pegram to divide his force, part of which, along with the cavalry, moved over to and up Vaughan Road, attacking the Federal left along Gravelly Run. The rest of Pegram's force maneuvered past Dabney's Sawmill only to encounter Crawford in his forward movement. Gregg's horsemen, supported by Griffin, were able to hold off the threat at Gravelly Run, but Crawford was not as lucky. Running into Pegram's other force, Crawford was first able to push the Confederates back to Dabney's sawdust pile, where they were reinforced by Evans' Division. A Union soldier recalled that at this point . . .

. . . the enemy's skirmishers were soon overtaken and pressed back upon the main line of Pegram's division . . . which also retired to the ruins of an old mill, where it made a stand. As the brigade came to an opening a formidable fort—as was supposed—presented itself in view, and a strife occurred between the color bearers of the 16th Maine and the 97th [New York] which should first plant its standard upon the fort. The 97th contestant achieved the victory; but great was his disappointment when instead of a veritable fort he found it only a huge heap of saw-dust.

During the fighting at this point, General Pegram was shot through the body near the heart, while "riding immediately with his troops." He died almost as soon as he touched the ground after being assisted from his mount. In turn, Crawford was forced back by the collapse of his left flank, held by the remains of the old Iron Brigade. Only by the arrival of Ayres to Crawford's support was the rout stopped. By this time the Confederates were preparing to make a counter-attack with further assistance from Finegan's (Mahone's) Division, which fell in between

John Pegram, CSA

Petersburg National Battlefield

Evans and Pegram, and upon doing so, Warren's line gave way and fell back to Vaughan Road. Nightfall brought an end to the action after Colonel James Hubbard's brigade, of Wheaton's division, was sent up to reinforce Warren's line. The colonel of the 61st Virginia under Finegan recalled the final charge on the 6th:

In the charge through the woods our ranks were broken by the undergrowth and trees, and the men were so much scattered, I went up to the general and suggested a halt to reform our line, which he did, and then moved forward in closed order to see the enemy seek shelter in his earthworks. . . . We were now drawn back to straighten and adjust our line of battle . . . the men hastily threw up scant breastworks for such are supposed to be high enough to kneel behind; these were scarcely high enough to lie behind, and as night was fast approaching our men made brush shelters to protect themselves as much as possible from the rain, snow, hail and sleet, but no fires could be allowed in such close proximity to the enemy. During the evening the cooks brought to the men in line of battle a small pone of bread each. . . .

Of the fighting that day, Colonel Morrow wrote that his brigade, upon being ordered to advance to the attack, did so "in good order but without that enthusiasm which I have been accustomed to find in my own Regiment [24th Michigan]— The advance was continued to the edge of a wood and beyond this the troops seemed disinclined to proceed— I made every exertion & got them further but with partial success. . . . I took the Brigade colors & advanced in front of the line and entreated the troops to follow— A few men and several officers came gallantly forward but the great mass did not." While doing so again at another point in the battle,

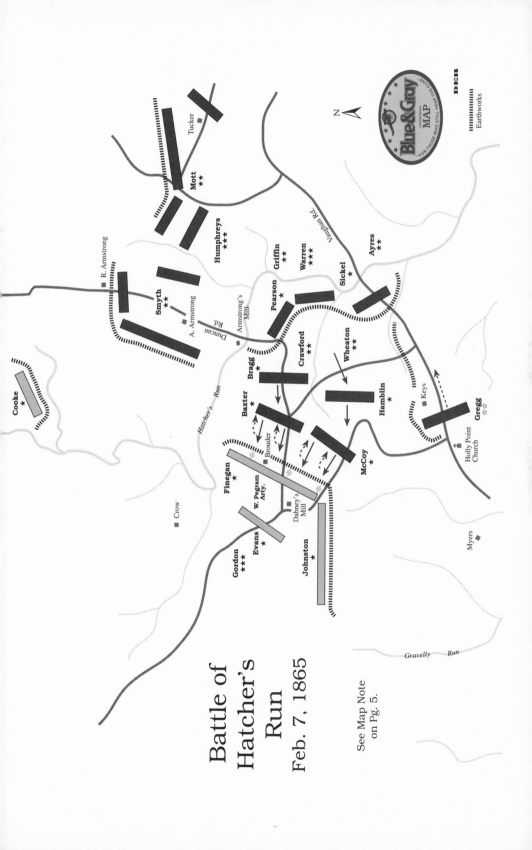

Morrow received a painful wound and left the field. He wrote later, "the night of the 6th was intensely cold and about 12 o'clock it began to snow & rain & continued to do this nearly all day of the 7th. On the morning of the 7th the earth was enveloped in a shroud of ice— As most of the severely wounded on our front line of battle were left on the field they all probably froze to death. . . ."

On the 7th General Warren once again went out to reconnoiter the area he had fought over the day before, and found the enemy entrenched near the sawmill. Only his skirmishers actually came in contact with the Confederates and no major attack was made. In the little fighting that did ensue, Confederate General Moxley Sorrel was wounded by a bullet through the lung. Gordon now had three small divisions holding his position: Finegan on the left, General Robert D. Johnston (commanding Pegram's) on the right, and Evans in support. Artillery, which throughout the battle was provided by the battalion of General Pegram's brother, Colonel William J. Pegram, was also adequately placed. As Colonel Morrow noted, snow and freezing rain hampered the operations of both armies this day, causing severe hardships for the men. Colonel William H. Stewart of the 61st Virginia recalled that the morning . . .

. . . broke clear, with long icicles hanging from the tree limbs, which bent under the burden like weeping willows, and the cold north wind was chilling and terrible to withstand. After daylight the soldiers were permitted to cut the sapling trees and build log fires, for they were almost at the freezing point. The men, shivering over these feeble fires, stood up the whole day like martyrs waiting for the enemy's attack. There was no activity in front until late in the afternoon, when the enemy opened fire upon us with artillery.

In the fighting on February 5-7, 1865, variably known as the Battle of Hatcher's Run, Armstrong's Mill, or Dabney's Mill (refer to the sketch on Pg. 167), the Federal loss amounted to 171 killed, 1,181 wounded and 187 missing. Confederate losses were estimated by a participant, Major Henry Kyd Douglas, at 1,000. Approximately 34,000 Federals were engaged in this offensive operation, while about 14,000 Confederate effectives were sent out to stop them. One Southerner remembered the battle as "preliminary skirmishing on the 5th, a sanguinary action on the 6th, followed up by the enemy feebly on the 7th." With this movement the Federals were now able to extend their trench system from Fort Sampson in the existing siege lines to the Vaughan Road crossing of Hatcher's Run. A Federal soldier wrote: "The result of the battle was important. It put our army in a position to attack the South Side railroad and cut off the avenue of Rebel supplies when we pleased, and at the same time it opened up to us an ample supply of fuel which had become scarce." Although the Federals had neither gained a foothold on the Boydton Plank Road nor cut the South Side Railroad, it put them about three miles closer to their goal than they had been previously.

It seems too that many of the Confederate soldiers suffered a lack of spirit in this engagement, as did some of Warren's Yankees. A Confederate deserter from Heth's Division told the Federals that on February 5, General Lee had addressed the divisions of Gordon, Mahone and Heth, which were facing the Union II Corps, and "that the orders to charge were repeatedly refused, and that General Lee wept like a child. Heth's Division afterward made three charges, with two lines of two brigades each." A possible reason for this lack of enthusiasm was addressed by General Lee on February 8, when he sent a letter to Secretary of War James Seddon. In it he remarked:

Yesterday, the most inclement day of the winter, [my men at Hatcher's Run] had to be retained in line of battle, having been in the same condition the two previous days and nights. I regret to be obliged to state that under these circumstances, heightened by assaults and fire of the enemy, some of the men had been without meat for three days, and all were suffering from reduced rations and scant clothing, exposed to battle, cold, hail, and sleet. . . . If some change is not made and the commissary department reorganized, I apprehend dire results.

Just a few days before, on February 6, General Robert E. Lee had been given command of all armies of the Confederacy, which, as one soldier wrote, was "at least two years too late" to make much difference. In Richmond, the arming of slaves was being hotly debated to fill Confederate ranks depleted by constant desertion and death. Jefferson Davis wrote that "we are reduced to choosing whether the negroes shall fight for us or against us. . . ." Both sides, it seems, were getting tired of the conflict, but an end would not come for another two months.

The Battle of Hatcher's Run was especially remembered in Petersburg for the loss of General John Pegram, a native son. He had married a lovely belle of Richmond, Hettie Cary, on January 19. The marriage was the talk of the Confederate capital, as he was considered "one of the handsomest and most lovable men" ever to wed "the handsomest woman in the Southland—with her classic face, her pure complexion, her auburn hair, her perfect figure and carriage. . . ." She was staying in Petersburg with her mother when his body arrived. Its bearer, Major Douglas, sadly noted "a fiancee of three years, a bride of three weeks, now a widow!" The happiness felt by civilians over the Pegram marriage, and the respite from war weariness it provided, had quickly come to an end.

Hettie Cary Pegram

Petersburg National Battlefield

The Yankees too had their sadness. During the fighting on the 6th, as the commander of the 24th Michigan was moving his men against the works at Dabney's Mill, he noticed some had ceased firing on one point in the line. They had stopped to bury the pet dog of the 11th Pennsylvania, whose name was "Sallie." Likely a mixed breed terrier, Sallie had been with the 11th regiment from its inception in 1861, when given to the men as a puppy. Following her comrades through all their campaigns, she always took her place beneath the flag in battle. After the Battle of Hatcher's Run, a member of the regiment wrote in a letter home: "Poor 'Sallie' fell in the front line in the fight at the Run—a bullet pierced her brain. She was buried where she fell by some of the boys even whilst under a murderous fire." He lamented later, "Sallie's bark will no longer be heard at the head of the column—her tail is wagless, and the marques, shelter tents and blankets that knew her shall know her no more forever— for her there is no more 'pomp and pride, and circumstances of glorious war.'"

Today the battlefield still holds much of its rural setting, but with frame and brick ranchers slowly dotting the landscape. Armstrong's Mill has been replaced by a structure known locally as Steere's Mill. With the millpond and dam, the structure provides a picturesque view of a time gone by. Vaughan Road still passes over Hatcher's Run where the Federals forced their crossing, but then diverts into what is called New Road. A dirt trace of the original road still runs toward Gravelly Run before petering out, while its intersection with the overgrown Dabney Mill Road is barely discernible. The site of Dabney's Steam-Saw-mill is now a garden spot at a bend in the present-day Dabney Mill Road, which is the former location of a wartime road intersection. Ironically, at one time it was marked by a mailbox with the local name "Pegram" emblazoned on it.

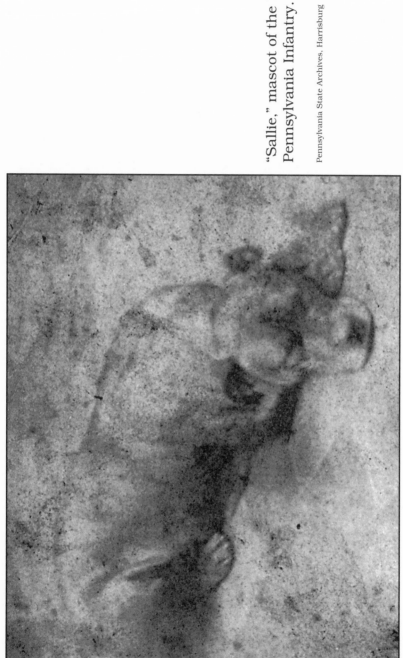

"Sallie," mascot of the 11th Pennsylvania Infantry.

Pennsylvania State Archives, Harrisburg

In recent years, preservation groups, such as the Association for the Preservation of Civil War Sites, and now the Civil War Preservation Trust, have acquired properties on this battlefield (refer to the Driving Tour, Pp. 163-168, for their locations). A Virginia State Historical marker and wayside exhibits now interpret the sites. These efforts have helped preserve for future generations the sacred soil where the gallant men in Blue & Gray struggled on those cold February days in 1865.

THE BATTLE OF FIVE FORKS

Final Push for the South Side

by Chris Calkins

Historian, Petersburg National Battlefield, Virginia

Maps prepared by Dave Roth of
Blue & Gray Magazine

Refer to the Tour Map on Pp. 136-137.

UNDER NORMAL CONDITIONS one could almost jump across Gravelly Run. But two days of heavy rains in Virginia had swollen this little creek far beyond its banks at the crossing of the Boydton Plank Road. The only solution for the Federal V Corps in getting across it was to construct a 40-foot bridge. This task was accomplished by two o'clock on the morning of April 1, 1865, as Gouverneur K. Warren's men began their race to join Phil Sheridan's cavalry near Dinwiddie Court House. Little did Warren realize that this day would end with a fight at a country crossroads that would prove to be his last battle in a war that was almost over. The Battle of Five Forks, termed "Waterloo of the Confederacy," would not only break the Siege of Petersburg, but cost this Northern general his place of glory in the final days of the war.

This spring movement, officially referred to in postwar years as the Appomattox Campaign, began on the slightly overcast morning of March 29, 1865. As had been the case since the previous September, the Federals' objectives were Lee's remaining supply lines into Petersburg: the Boydton Plank Road and the South Side Railroad. A few days earlier, General Ulysses S. Grant had met with his various corps commanders to outline his spring operational plans. Warren's V Corps was to move to the junction of Quaker and Vaughan roads and await the arrival of Andrew A. Humphreys' II Corps. Humphreys was to

Philip H. Sheridan, USA

go into position with Quaker Road on his left and Hatcher's Run on his right as Warren advanced to and along the Boydton Plank Road. General Sheridan, whose men had just arrived from the Shenandoah Valley, was to strike for Dinwiddie Court House and attempt to entice the Confederates to leave their breastworks and fight in the open. If this did not happen, Sheridan could break away from the main army and attempt to destroy portions of the South Side and Richmond & Danville railroads to the west.

To support this movement west of Hatcher's Run, Grant secretly withdrew portions of General Edward O. C. Ord's Army of the James from the north side of the James River and sent them to the southwest of Petersburg. These troops were to hold the sections of the line abandoned by the II Corps. Ord brought with him his small cavalry division (formerly August Kautz's) led by the young brigadier, Ranald S. Mackenzie, top graduate in the West Point Class of 1862. In the siege lines north of Ord was General Horatio G. Wright's VI Corps, then General John G. Parke's IX Corps near the Jerusalem Plank Road.

Leaving their winter camps south of Petersburg, Warren's corps marched in a southwesterly direction and, after crossing Rowanty Creek on pontoon bridges at the Stage Road, proceeded to the intersection of Vaughan and Quaker roads. On reaching that point, Warren received a series of contradictory messages from General George G. Meade, commander of the Army of the Potomac, telling him to proceed up the Quaker Road instead of the Boydton Plank Road.

Meanwhile, farther south, Sheridan's cavalry was on the road. Leaving their camps along the Jerusalem Plank Road at Hancock's Station, they rode south past Gary's Church then through Reams' Station, eventually turning west at Malone's Crossing on the Weldon Railroad. Shortly thereafter they too had to

Gouverneur K. Warren, USA

cross the Rowanty at Malone's Bridge. General George Crook's division (3,300 men) was in the lead, followed by Generals George A. Custer's and Thomas C. Devin's divisions (5,700 men); the latter two reported to General Wesley Merritt. The cavalry had a hard go of it this day as the wagons and horses quickly turned the sand and clay soil of the area into a quagmire. When the horsemen reached Malone's Bridge they found that the Confederate outpost on the opposite bank had burned the structure. The cavalry's progress was much slower than the Federal infantry, which was marching ahead of its wagons on the other route.

Of course, all this did not go unnoticed by General Robert E. Lee. He realized that Grant's men were going after the South Side Railroad and that the Federals would probably head for the upper reaches of Hatcher's Run and move around Lee's right flank. Examining local maps, Lee felt that the route the Federals would use was by way of Dinwiddie Court House and Five Forks. The problem facing the Confederate commander was that the important road junction of Five Forks was four miles west of where Lee's right flank rested on Claiborne Road. This unprotected zone was beyond his already 30-plus miles of entrenchments. Protecting this vital right flank, running from Burgess' Mill on the Boydton Plank Road to Hatcher's Run on Claiborne Road, was General Richard H. Anderson's corps, consisting of only General Bushrod Johnson's division (about 4,800 men) and Colonel Hilary P. Jones' four battalions of artillery.

Lee decided the best way to thwart Grant's menacing operation was to put together a mobile force composed of infantry and cavalry. He called for the cavalry divisions under his son, Rooney Lee, and the army commander's nephew, General Fitzhugh Lee. Fitz Lee's forces, numbering around 1,800, were stationed a two days' march away on the north side of the James River. Forty miles to the southeast, at

Stony Creek Station on the Weldon Railroad, were Rooney Lee's 2,400 horsemen. They were reinforced by General Thomas L. Rosser's division of approximately 1,200 troopers.

For the infantry command, Robert E. Lee chose the division of General George E. Pickett. Having had a relatively calm nine months during the Petersburg siege, Pickett's troops held what was called the "Howlett Line" at Bermuda Hundred between the James and Appomattox rivers. Although Pickett's men had seen very little activity on this front, there seemed to be a high number of desertions in the ranks. The division was composed of the brigades of Generals Montgomery D. Corse and William R. Terry, which held the Howlett Line; General George H. Steuart's brigade in Petersburg, having been called there during the Battle of Fort Stedman on March 25; and Pickett's last brigade, under General Eppa Hunton, north of the James. Pickett had about 5,000 men.

Back at his headquarters just outside Petersburg, Robert E. Lee hurried these forces into position. Fitz Lee was sent via Cox Road to Sutherland Station on the South Side, ten miles west of the city, where Rooney Lee and Tom Rosser were to meet him. It was at this time that Fitz Lee was verbally given command of all the Army of Northern Virginia's cavalry. He was to seize the initiative and attack Sheridan's forces in the Dinwiddie Court House vicinity.

Meanwhile, Pickett put his infantrymen in motion with Corse and Terry crossing the Appomattox River and joining with Steuart in Petersburg. They were then sent by train to Sutherland Station, arriving late on the 29th. Hunton's brigade stayed near Manchester (across the James River from Richmond) in the event they were needed to guard the railroad. To bolster Anderson's Corps along White Oak Road, Lee sent General Samuel McGowan's brigade of Cadmus Wilcox's division.

The Battle of Lewis' Farm

While Sheridan was on the road with 9,000 troopers, heading for Dinwiddie Court House, Warren began his march northward up Quaker Road. The vanguard of his column, General Joshua L. Chamberlain's brigade, ran into its first resistance as the brigade approached Gravelly Run. The men were to push on to the Boydton Plank Road and hold it, along with anchoring their right on the II Corps' left flank. Fording the waist-deep run, Chamberlain threw out skirmishers and advanced his two large regiments, the 198th Pennsylvania and 185th New York. Upon reaching a farmhouse owned by the Lewis family, a large contingent of the enemy was seen beyond some sawdust piles near a sawmill at the edge of a clearing. Chamberlain halted his brigade until reinforcements arrived, in the form of Colonel Edgar M. Gregory's brigade, which went in on Chamberlain's left.

The Southern troops Chamberlain saw in the clearing were from General Henry A. Wise's Virginia brigade, sent from the White Oak Road lines by Bushrod Johnson. As Chamberlain advanced his battleline the fighting began in earnest. Slowly Wise's men fell back a mile toward the junction of the Boydton Plank Road and Quaker Road. Seeing this retrograde movement, Anderson deployed General William H. Wallace's South Carolinians, who fell in on the right of Wise. Together the two brigades counterattacked and brought Chamberlain's advance to a halt. After fierce fighting for almost a half-hour the Federal left flank began to give ground.

About this time Union artillery, which had just crossed Gravelly Run, came on the scene. Battery B, 4th U. S. Light Artillery unlimbered its four pieces, with a section (two guns) on each side of the Lewis house. It was none too soon, as the Confederates were quickly closing in on the position. Loading canister

Battle of Lewis' Farm
(or Quaker Road)
Mar. 29, 1865

THE UNION ATTACK

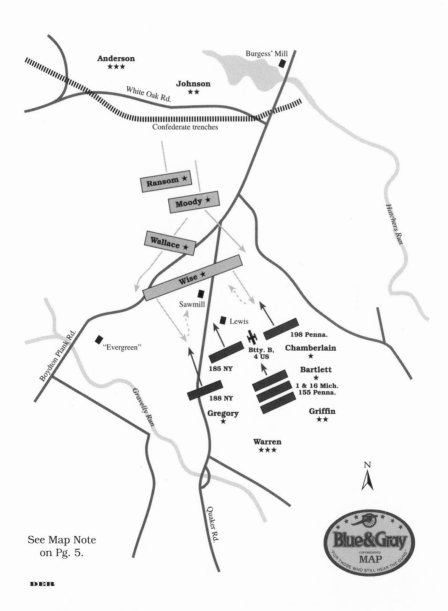

See Map Note
on Pg. 5.

DER

into two of the Napoleons on the west side of the dwelling, Federal cannoneers raked Wise's line.

Bushrod Johnson observed the situation and ordered General Young M. Moody's Alabama brigade to attack on Wise's left. The men went in on the double-quick, with General Matthew W. Ransom's North Carolinians remaining in support. With three Confederate brigades attacking Chamberlain's line, the general knew he could not hold much longer. After sending a plea for help, Chamberlain's division commander, General Charles Griffin, sent him four regiments: the 1st and 16th Michigan regiments, the 155th Pennsylvania Zouaves of General Joseph J. Bartlett's brigade, and the 188th New York from Gregory's.

Early in the fight, near the sawdust piles, Chamberlain narrowly escaped death. A bullet meant for him struck his horse's neck, which bore the brunt of the projectile's force. The bullet then struck the general's arm and followed it to the elbow, bruising it, before hitting his left breast just below the heart. Glancing off a leather case of field orders and a brass-mounted hand mirror, the bullet followed around two ribs and came out the back seam of Chamberlain's coat. Although a painful wound, the Maine general stayed at his post throughout the campaign.

As fresh troops arrived to support Chamberlain, they pressed forward past the Lewis house to the sawdust piles, using them as breastworks. Johnson's men began to give ground and fell back to the woods along the edge of the clearing.

Anderson, realizing the Federals were now bolstered with fresh troops, recalled Wise's, Wallace's and Moody's men to the White Oak Road entrenchments. Shortly, Union skirmishers gained the junction of the Boydton Plank and Quaker roads. The remainder of Griffin's division followed and began building entrenchments. Samuel W. Crawford's division was

Battle of Lewis' Farm
(or Quaker Road)
Mar. 29, 1865

SITUATION AFTER THE BATTLE

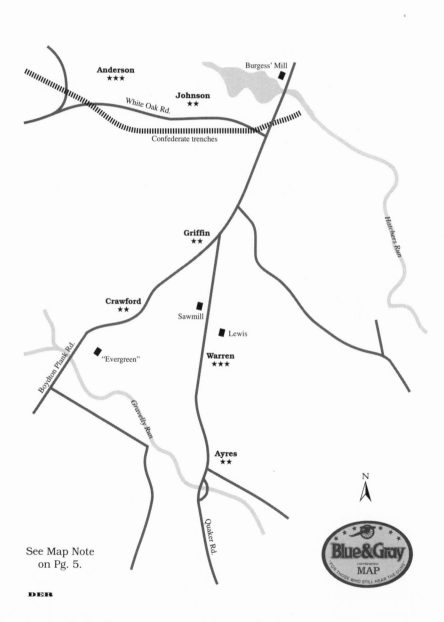

Anderson ★★★

Burgess' Mill

Johnson ★★

White Oak Rd.

Confederate trenches

Hatchers Run

Griffin ★★

Crawford ★★

Sawmill

Lewis

"Evergreen"

Warren ★★★

Boydton Plank Rd.

Gravelly Run

Ayres ★★

N

Quaker Rd.

Blue & Gray
COPYRIGHTED
MAP
"FOR THOSE WHO STILL HEAR THE GUNS"

See Map Note
on Pg. 5.

DER

ordered up a country lane that led in a northwest direction where he too reached the Boydton Plank Road. His men connected with Griffin's left. Romeyn B. Ayres' division stayed near the Quaker Road crossing of Gravelly Run.

The engagement at Lewis' Farm enabled the Federals to gain a foothold on one of Lee's supply routes, the Boydton Plank Road. The Confederate loss was estimated at 371, mostly from Wise's and Wallace's brigades. General Griffin said he captured 200 Southerners, and his men buried 130 of the enemy on the battlefield. Union casualties were 53 killed, 306 wounded, and 22 missing, for a total of 381.

When General Lee heard of the setback on Anderson's front he dispatched Hunton's Brigade to Anderson's assistance. Lee also ordered Colonel William J. "Willie" Pegram's 20-gun artillery battalion to Burgess' Mill. Feeling he might be needed at this threatened point in his lines, on the 30th Lee rode out to Sutherland Station to confer with his officers. General Lee decided that Pickett should take Corse's, Terry's and Steuart's brigades, along with two of Johnson's (Ransom's and Wallace's) and march to Five Forks. At that point they would rendezvous with Fitz Lee's cavalry and move on Dinwiddie Court House. Marching via Claiborne Road, by 9:45 p.m. on the 30th Pickett's division was along White Oak Road, its right flank at Five Forks.

General Grant, pleased with the day's success on the 29th, ordered Sheridan to forego his railroad raid and "push round the enemy . . . and get on his right rear." Warren spent the next day cautiously advancing Ayres' and Crawford's divisions toward Confederate lines on White Oak Road, while Humphreys' II Corps pushed forward after making contact with the V Corps' right on the night of the 29th. After sizing up the deployment of his troops, Grant sent another dispatch to Sheridan:

Andrew A. Humphreys, USA

If your situation in the morning [March 31] is such as to justify the belief that you can turn the enemy's right with the assistance of a corps of infantry, entirely detached from the balance of the army, I will so detach the Fifth Corps, and place the whole under your command for the operation.

Sheridan, whose troopers were then riding into Dinwiddie Court House, replied that he would prefer Wright's VI Corps (probably because Sheridan had worked well with that corps in the Shenandoah Valley the previous autumn) and "would not like the V Corps to make such an attempt." Grant replied that because Wright's troops were in a favorable position where they were, the VI Corps could not be sent. Warren's V Corps was available, and that's the infantry corps Sheridan got.

Fighting at White Oak Road

General Warren spent most of the 30th holding his position and issuing three days' rations to his men. The II Corps did likewise. Ayres' division was massed closest to White Oak Road, just south and west of the Claiborne Road junction. Ayres had reached that point by following a woods road that led from the Boydton Plank Road and crossed a branch of Gravelly Run, which was more than three feet deep from heavy rains. Crawford followed and covered Ayres' right flank near the Holliday house. Griffin stayed on the high ground overlooking the south bank of the run, at Mrs. Butler's place, along the Boydton Plank Road. All of the V Corps was now west of this roadway.

Since Ayres' left flank extended about three quarters of a mile west of the point where the Confederate works veered to the north at White Oak and Claiborne roads, Warren realized the opportunity

Battle of
White Oak Road
Mar. 31, 1865

PHASE 1

Claiborne Rd.

Hatchers Run

Anderson
★★★

Jones

Johnson
★★

Burgess' Mill

Hyman
★

White Oak Rd.

Butler

Dabney

Confederate trenches

Hunton
★

Wise
★

Stansel ★

McGowan ★

Ayres ★★

Mott

Crawford ★★

Humphreys
★★★

Miles ★★

Boydton Plank Rd.

**Btty. H,
1 NY**

Mrs.
Butler

Sawmill

Griffin ★★

Lewis

Warren
★★★
"Evergreen"
V Corps HQ

Bridge
out

Gravelly Run

See Map Note
on Pg. 5.

N

Blue&Gray
COPYRIGHTED
MAP
"FOR THOSE WHO STILL HEAR THE GUNS"

Quaker Rd.

DER

he had. Sending a message to Meade at 4:00 p.m., Warren told him he could "block the White Oak road"—which would keep Anderson from sending any troops to the west in support of Pickett at Five Forks.

On the morning of the 31st, Robert E. Lee himself rode to the White Oak Road lines to inspect them and confer with his generals. Meeting Johnson at the "return" (where the trenches curved north to Hatcher's Run at the White Oak Road-Claiborne Road junction), Lee learned that the Federals were in front and that their left flank was exposed. Deciding to seize the initiative, Lee chose four brigades for an attack: Moody and Wise (of Johnson's division), Hunton (Pickett's), and McGowan (Wilcox's). General Johnson was in immediate command of the operation, but he served under the supervision of Richard Anderson.

The Confederates slipped out of their works early on the morning of the 31st and formed in the woods on the north side of White Oak Road. McGowan was on the far right, then Moody (who was sick, so Colonel Martin L. Stansel was in command), and Hunton; Wise was held in reserve on Hunton's left.

Meanwhile, over in Ayres' command, his brigades were preparing for their assault. In the lead were Colonel Frederic Winthrop's New Yorkers. *En echelon* on Winthrop's right was Colonel James Gwyn's brigade, and covering the left flank was Colonel Andrew W. Denison's brigade of Marylanders. At 10:30 a.m. Ayres sent Winthrop's brigade forward to take White Oak Road and entrench upon it. Advancing across Halter Butler's field south of the road, muskets blazed from the woods on the opposite side. The Federals, coming within 10-15 yards of the road, saw that the Confederates were taking the initiative.

Bushrod Johnson ordered his command to advance. Lieutenant John Holland, 18th Virginia Infantry of Hunton's brigade, jumped up with sword in hand and yelled "Forward!" Although they had not quite

Richard H. Anderson, CSA

gotten into position, McGowan's South Carolinians assailed Ayres' left flank, sending Winthrop's men in full retreat. The sudden burst of Southern boldness caused Gwyn to do likewise and his troops fell back on Crawford's division. McGowan finally hit Denison, whose troops were held up in a ravine. After holding his position a short time, the breaking of the other two brigades eventually caused Denison's Marylanders to retreat; the men did not stop until they reached the branch of Gravelly Run. Denison was wounded during the retreat but refused to leave the field. Ayres' shattered division scampered across Gravelly Run.

Four Confederate brigades had broken over 5,000 men of the V Corps and sent them in full retreat. Crawford then formed his brigades for the impending attack. The Federals tried in vain to hold back the Southerners, but their momentum was too great. Eventually Crawford's men fell back across Gravelly Run, like Ayres' before them. The pursuing Confederates stopped just short of the stream. A member of the 18th Virginia, Sam Paulette, remembered the role of Hunton's brigade:

The Yanks came charging over the hill and closed on our skirmish line in a hurry. A Lieutenant of the 8th [?] Virginia regiment, seeing the danger to the line in front, called out in a loud voice: "Boys, they will capture our skirmishers; charge them." Without further orders, the boys raised the old yell, and at them we went on the run, with guns at the trail. Nearing them we opened fire, but continued to advance. The boys in blue stood it for a while, but finding that we were closing in for a hand-to-hand fight, they broke and ran, we at their heels yelling like devils, and burning powder for all we were worth. Running them into a large body of woods, we found another line formed to meet us. We did not stop, but charged

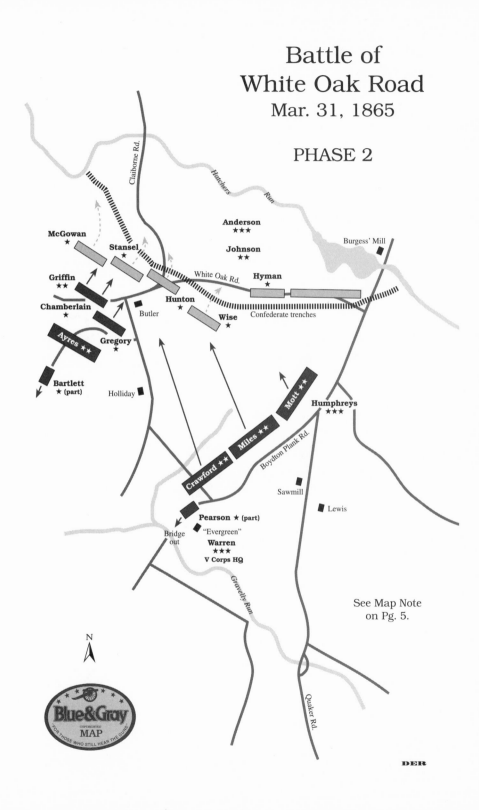

Battle of
White Oak Road
Mar. 31, 1865

PHASE 2

Claiborne Rd.

Hatchers Run

Anderson
★★★

Burgess' Mill

Johnson
★★

McGowan
★

Stansel

Griffin
★★

White Oak Rd.

Hyman
★

Chamberlain
★

Hunton
★

Butler

Wise
★

Confederate trenches

Ayres ★★★

Gregory
★

Bartlett
★ (part)

Holliday

Mott ★★★

Humphreys
★★★

Miles ★★

Crawford ★★

Boydton Plank Rd.

Sawmill

Lewis

Pearson ★ (part)

Bridge
out

"Evergreen"

Warren
★★★
V Corps HQ

Gravelly Run

See Map Note
on Pg. 5.

N

Blue&Gray
COPYRIGHTED
MAP
FOR THOSE WHO STILL HEAR THE GUNS

Quaker Rd.

DER

. . . and broke this line also, and continued to ad-
vance. About a quarter-mile from this point we dis-
covered their third line. By this time we were all bro-
ken up, and orders came to halt and reform the line,
which we did in a few minutes although under fire.
Orders now came to charge the third line, which we
did in fine style, breaking it up in short order. We
now had three lines of battle of the enemy, running
in our front, we following on the run, yelling, shoot-
ing and killing all we could. This was all very nice,
and we enjoyed it, but the Yanks' time was now to
come.

Back in the main Confederate lines Lee awaited
the outcome of the attack. He also ordered Wise's
Brigade to fall in on Hunton's left. Then Lee, along
with General McGowan, rode forward and met with
Bushrod Johnson. After determining that without reinforcements their position would become untenable,
they ordered the men to fall back to a small line of
works that Ayres' men had thrown up south of White
Oak Road earlier. By 3:00 p.m. the Southerners had
completed this movement and set about reversing the
face of the entrenchments.

At Griffin's camp overlooking the run, the sight
of disorganized Federals told of the disaster. The general had the "long roll" beaten and ordered his men
to fall in. Four Napoleons of Battery H, 1st New York
Light Artillery, were set up on the high ground and
opened fire as the Confederates came in view. When
Warren learned what had happened to Ayres' and
Crawford's divisions, he sent a staff officer to General Humphreys and asked the II Corps commander
to send help. In response, General Nelson A. Miles
with two brigades fell in on Warren's right.

By 2:30 Ayres and Crawford had reformed their
commands and Warren gave the order for a second
advance. This time Griffin took charge. He asked

Bushrod R. Johnson, CSA

Chamberlain if he felt able to command the attack, since Chamberlain was still suffering from his March 29th wounds. Never one to shy away from danger, the general replied in the affirmative. His goal was to regain the ground lost earlier by Ayres and Crawford and press toward White Oak Road. Crossing the waist-deep branch of Gravelly Run, Chamberlain pushed his two regiments forward, followed closely by Gregory's brigade, which formed on his right. General Bartlett then crossed and fell in on Chamberlain's left-rear; Ayres' division supported Griffin's left while Crawford supported his right. Confederate Sam Paulette remembered . . .

. . . our boys, having already broken three lines of battle, were very much scattered, and before we could line them up, the Yanks charged. It was impossible in our condition, to successfully resist this counter-charge, and the boys began to fall back; slowly at first. The Yanks, seeing how few we were, began to crowd us, and we broke into a run, and made back to our start-ing-point, and, this being the Yanks' time, they gave us "hail Columbia" before we reached the White Oak Swamp [sic] Road. . . .

While Chamberlain had no problem pushing back the few small groups of Confederates he encountered, it was not until he ran into Hunton's entire force that he was stopped. These troops were the ones which had taken refuge behind the line of works thrown up earlier by Ayres' troops. These slight entrenchments, which the Rebels had "turned," were south of White Oak Road and generally parallel to the main Confederate line. With the 198th Pennsylvania in advance, Chamberlain charged the Confederates after receiving orders from Griffin. As his men surged toward the field where the initial Southern counterattack had taken place that morning, they ran into a deadly

Joshua L. Chamberlain, USA

crossfire from enemy troops posted in the woods, causing some of the men to waver. At the same time, they received a fierce shelling from Hilary Jones' artillery emplaced in two redans near the bend in the main Confederate breastworks. Calling for assistance, Gregory's brigade came up in support as Chamberlain drove Hunton's men out of Ayres' old breastworks, cutting off and capturing most of the 56th Virginia.

Eppa Hunton recalled that "the Federal line wavered under the fire very decidedly, and a portion of it broke and ran. The balance of the line re-formed under my fire, advanced, and drove us back. I thought it was one of the most gallant things I had ever seen." At this point the remainder of the Virginians withdrew into the main line as the Federals gained White Oak Road. It was 3:40 in the afternoon. McGowan's South Carolinians, cut off from the rest of the army by Chamberlain and Gregory, had to return to their defenses by a roundabout way.

General Warren arrived on the scene and made a personal reconnaissance, hoping he could attack Anderson's line at the curve in the breastworks. As Warren was doing this his soldiers began strengthening their newly-won ground by throwing up more entrenchments. After making his examination of the enemy lines, Warren, who was a skilled engineer, concluded "that the foe's defenses were as complete and as well located as any . . . [I] had ever been opposed to [and] that it would be useless to sacrifice the men in an assault."

The engagement at White Oak Road, sometimes referred to as the Battle of Gravelly Run, or Hatcher's Run (which flowed behind the Confederate lines), effectively prevented Anderson's Corps (Johnson's division) from reinforcing Pickett's force at Five Forks. To reach that point, Anderson would now have to send his troops on a long, circuitous route via Sutherland Station and the South Side Railroad. With

Samuel McGowan, CSA

Warren's corps in their front, even that would be nearly impossible.

The fight at White Oak Road cost the Union army 177 killed, 1,134 wounded and 554 missing, for a total of 1,865; 1,407 of those were from the V Corps, the rest being from Miles' division of Humphreys' II Corps which supported Warren's right flank. Confederate General Bushrod Johnson, whose force numbered between 4,500-5,000 men, put his losses at "about 800, including killed, wounded and missing." He also claimed his forces captured about 470 Federals. Warren reported that he captured 118 prisoners and buried 126 dead Rebels.

Around 5:00 p.m. General Warren received a message from General Meade's headquarters instructing him to secure and protect his position, and to send a small force to the west to try and communicate with Sheridan's forces. Warren readied Bartlett's brigade for this purpose.

The Battle of Dinwiddie Court House

Dinwiddie County, formed in 1752 and named for Governor Richard Dinwiddie, had been the center of Federal operations against Petersburg since August 1864, when the Weldon Railroad was cut by the Yankee army. Running along the eastern boundary of the county, this railroad provided Lee with an important supply link to North Carolina. When he could no longer use it directly into Petersburg, Lee was forced to detrain his war materiel at a safe point along the line and find an alternative transportation route. This Lee accomplished by using a wagon train which passed through Dinwiddie Court House and moved into Petersburg via the Boydton Plank Road. One of Sheridan's troopers described Dinwiddie Court House as . . .

George G. Meade, USA

. . . a small village, about thirteen miles from Petersburg . . . and, although the county seat, it seemed to have contained when in its prime not over a half a dozen dwellings. Most of them were now deserted; all looked very uncomfortable and dilapidated, the most inviting one being a roomy, large frame building, of country-tavern appearance, with a long portico in front, adapted to the use of three-legged chairs and tobacco-spitting loungers. Conveniently situated, close to the roadside, it commands, in a most appropriate connection, an excellent view of the court-house and jail opposite. . . . The court-house betokened a more modern appearance than the specimens of rural architecture surrounding it, and was built of red brick, freshly painted. The roof, as though tottering under the unusual burden of new repairs and improvements thereupon, was bolstered up by immense timbers supporting its eaves. The court-room, in the upper story, formed a most excellent dormitory, and the various legal and county offices, on the first floor, gave employment to many a wandering soldier. The floors were irreverently strewn with abstracts of title, venerable mortgages, copies of deeds, and other such interesting matter as appertains to a county clerk's office. This being one of the oldest counties in Virginia, many of the documents were yellow with age, some bearing the date as far back as the time of Governor Dinwiddie, and, for aught I know, furnishing golden opportunities to the American antiquarian.

Close by the court-house stood a neat little frame church [probably Calvary Episcopal Church, which the 1st Maine Cavalry would later use as a hospital], prettily trimmed inside with evergreen and with neat appointments. Respected by the soldiers, the church, though much occupied as a convenient shelter from the storm, was more fortunate than its neighboring buildings, and escaped serious injury.

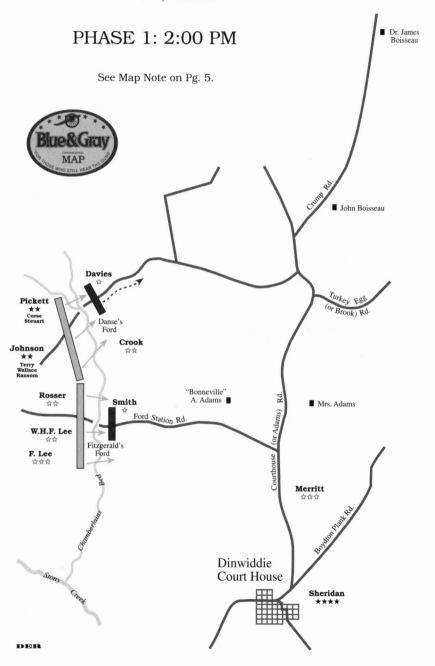

Battle of
Dinwiddie Court House
Mar. 31, 1865

PHASE 1: 2:00 PM

See Map Note on Pg. 5.

Blue&Gray
COPYRIGHTED
MAP
FOR THOSE WHO STILL HEAR THE GUNS

N

Dr. James
Boisseau

Crump Rd.

John Boisseau

Davies
☆

Pickett
★★
Corse
Steuart

Danse's
Ford

Turkey Egg
(or Brook) Rd.

Crook
☆☆

Johnson
★★
Terry
Wallace
Ransom

Rosser
☆☆

Smith
☆

"Bonneville"
A. Adams ■

Mrs. Adams

Ford Station Rd.

Courthouse (or Adams) Rd.

W.H.F. Lee
☆☆

Fitzgerald's
Ford

F. Lee
☆☆☆

Merritt
☆☆☆

Chamberlains Bed

Boydton Plank Rd.

Stony Creek

Dinwiddie
Court House

Sheridan
★★★★

DER

. . . Sheridan planted his headquarters flag in front of the venerable tavern, and with himself and staff thus, as a matter of course, "put up" at the best hotel in the town.

Friday, March 31, was a day which saw two contests: Warren and his V Corps' push for White Oak Road and their clash with Anderson's men, and Sheridan's cavalry being struck in the area of Dinwiddie Court House by Pickett's force. Early that morning, Wesley Merritt of Sheridan's command sent patrols up the numerous roads leading to Five Forks from Dinwiddie Court House. These included Courthouse Road (also known as Adams Road up to the fork with Crump Road), Crump Road, and Ford's Road; the latter led in a westward direction from Courthouse Road and crossed Chamberlain's Bed, a small, swampy tributary which fed into nearby Stony Creek. Pickett marched his combined force of infantry and cavalry south from Five Forks along Scott's Road toward Ford's Road. At the point where the two roads intersected, known as Little Five Forks, the Confederate column turned southeast toward Chamberlain's Bed. If Pickett were successful he would be able to turn Sheridan's left flank. To harass Federal cavalry patrolling around Five Forks, Pickett left behind Colonel Thomas T. Munford's horsemen with instructions to hold White Oak Road at that point. If he heard firing from Pickett's force, Munford was to attack Sheridan's troopers along Courthouse Road.

The capture of some enemy soldiers alerted Sheridan to Pickett's operation. Sheridan quickly dispatched General Henry E. Davies and Colonel Charles H. Smith, whose brigades were in Crook's division, to cover the two crossings over Chamberlain's Bed at Danse's and Fitzgerald's fords. As the Confederates approached the fords at about 2:00 p.m., Pickett made final dispositions for the attack. Fitz Lee, with Rooney

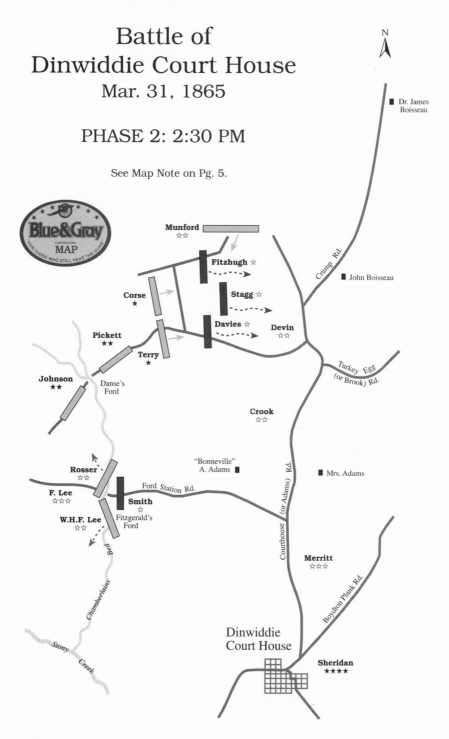

Battle of
Dinwiddie Court House
Mar. 31, 1865

PHASE 2: 2:30 PM

See Map Note on Pg. 5.

N

Blue&Gray
COPYRIGHTED
MAP
FOR THOSE WHO STILL HEAR THE GUNS

Dr. James
Boisseau

Munford
☆☆

Fitzhugh ☆

Corse
★

Stagg ☆

Crump Rd.

John Boisseau

Pickett
★★

Davies ☆

Devin
☆☆

Terry
★

Johnson
★★

Danse's
Ford

Turkey Egg
(or Brook) Rd.

Crook
☆☆

"Bonneville"
A. Adams

Rosser
☆☆

Ford Station Rd.

Mrs. Adams

F. Lee
☆☆☆

Smith
☆

W.H.F. Lee
☆☆

Fitzgerald's
Ford

Courthouse (or Adams) Rd.

Merritt
☆☆☆

Chamberlains Bed

Boydton Plank Rd.

Stony Creek

Dinwiddie
Court House

Sheridan
★★★★

DER

Lee's and Tom Rosser's cavalry, were to force a passage at Fitzgerald's Ford, while Pickett and the infantry crossed farther north at Danse's Ford. Although the attack was meant to be a coordinated one, for some reason the cavalry pushed forward without waiting for Pickett and battle was joined prematurely.

Smith's Yankee cavalry, outnumbered, fought valiantly to stem the Confederate onslaught, at one point even crossing the neck-deep swamp to grapple with the enemy only to be thrown back in confusion. As the fighting swayed back and forth across Chamberlain's Bed, Rosser received a slight wound. Eventually the firing died down as Smith and his men dug in along some bluffs to the east. It was not until after five o'clock, while under enemy artillery fire, that Smith received word that Confederate infantry had crossed at Danse's Ford and was threatening his right flank.

The first of Pickett's infantry across at Danse's Ford was Corse's Virginia brigade. At this time only a small battalion from Davies' command was there to meet them. It seems that Davies had taken a good portion of his men south to reinforce Smith, but finding Smith holding his own, Davies immediately counter-marched his men northward to the sound of the guns. Arriving just in time, Davies' brigade attempted to stop the Southern infantry, but was unsuccessful. General Davies ordered his men to fall back to Courthouse (or Adams) Road.

Meanwhile, south of Five Forks, Munford was pursuing Thomas Devin's two brigades, under Colonels Peter Stagg and Charles L. Fitzhugh, as they fell back to join the rest of Sheridan's cavalry. Hearing the fire of Davies' men to the south, Devin sent his command to their support; they fell in on Davies' right flank. With this added Union firepower, Pickett was forced to add another brigade to help Corse. This proved to be another group of Virginians, under William R.

Battle of
Dinwiddie Court House
Mar. 31, 1865

N

PHASE 3: 4:00-5:30 PM

See Map Note on Pg. 5.

■ Dr. James
Boisseau

Blue&Gray
COPYRIGHTED
MAP
FOR THOSE WHO STILL HEAR THE GUNS

Crump Rd.

■ John Boisseau

Johnson
★★

Munford
☆☆

Corse
★

Danse's
Ford

Terry
★

Pickett
★★

Turkey Egg
(or Brook) Rd.

Gibbs
☆

Gregg
☆

"Bonneville"
A. Adams
■

Rosser
☆☆

Ford Station Rd.

F. Lee
☆☆☆

■ Mrs. Adams

Fitzgerald's
Ford

W.H.F. Lee
☆☆

Smith
☆

Courthouse (or Adams) Rd.

Merritt
☆☆☆

Crook
☆☆

Sheridan
★★★★

Boydton Plank Rd.

Davies
☆

Dinwiddie
Court House

Fitzhugh
☆

Stagg
☆

Devin
☆☆

Chamberlains Bed

Stony Creek

DER

Terry. At the same time, Munford's cavalry arrived on the scene and attacked Colonel Fitzhugh's right flank. The Southerners were able to press the Federals back to Courthouse Road where Crump Road branched off at the Boisseau (pronounced Boy-saw) place. As Sheridan's men tried to reform at this point, Pickett was able to get some of his troops to Courthouse Road, between Davies and Devin, and cut them off from the rest of the Federal command at Dinwiddie Court House. When General Merritt realized the predicament his men were in, he sent word for them to ride eastward until they reached the Boydton Plank Road. If they could do that, and the Confederates continued their push on Dinwiddie Court House, they might soon find themselves in a position to attack Pickett's left flank and rear.

Between Pickett's force and Devin's, and covering the junction of Turkey Egg Road (also known as Brook Road) and Courthouse Road, was General Alfred Gibbs' brigade of Devin's division. General Devin attempted to hook up with his remaining brigade via the plank road but was ordered to Dinwiddie Court House instead, with Davies. Upon their arrival they went into camp on the outskirts of the village. Colonel J. Irvin Gregg's brigade of Crook's cavalry, originally held in reserve, was sent forward to help Gibbs. At the same time, word was sent to General Custer to send two of his brigades to Dinwiddie while the other one guarded the wagon train in the rear.

Pickett swung his infantry battleline around so that it faced south toward Dinwiddie Court House. Terry and Corse had their left flank covered by Munford's cavalry, which joined them from the Five Forks area. The Confederates continued to press Gibbs' and Gregg's lines of dismounted cavalry, but the Federal troopers were able to hold their ground for about two hours before Gibbs was forced to fall back due to a withering enemy fire.

Wesley Merritt, USA

By 5:30 p.m. Custer's two brigades, under Colonels Alexander C. M. Pennington and Henry Capehart, arrived on the scene and went into position about a half-mile north of Dinwiddie Court House. As they did, Gibbs' and Gregg's brigades came in from their position and Gregg fell in on Pennington's right. Gibbs continued on to Dinwiddie. Because Colonel Smith's brigade was exposed by this move, he too left his position along Chamberlain's Bed and formed on Capehart's left. Custer's line was bolstered with four 3-inch rifles of Battery A, 2nd U. S. Light Artillery.

Now that Smith no longer held Fitzgerald's Ford, Rooney Lee and Rosser pushed across and connected with Pickett's right flank. As the line of combined infantry and cavalry pressed forward toward Dinwiddie they encountered Custer's line. Pickett decided he would attack them on their front while Fitz Lee struck the Federal left. The Confederates first came in contact with Pennington, since his brigade was in advance of Custer's main position. Falling back in front of the deadly musket fire, Pennington reformed his line with the others and had his troopers throw up a line of fence-rail breastworks along a ridge. Assailed twice by Pickett's infantry, the horse soldiers held their ground, then made a counterattack and threw Pickett's skirmishers back. Smith's brigade, hit by Fitz Lee's troopers, also held its ground, until darkness fell and Smith withdrew. Apparently most of his brigade had run out of ammunition from the day's fighting. As night came over the battlefield, the opposing forces rested within easy sight of one another. The Confederates held the high ground on the Abner Adams farm, "Bonneville," while Custer's men were dug in along a ridge just north of the village.

Tactically the Battle of Dinwiddie Court House was a victory for George E. Pickett. He had stopped Sheridan's advance on Five Forks dead in its tracks.

Battle of Dinwiddie Court House
Mar. 31, 1865

PHASE 4: 5:30 PM

See Map Note on Pg. 5.

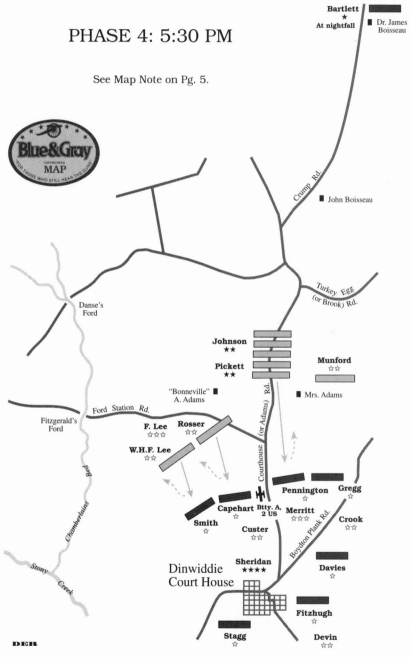

DER

Reaching that important road junction would not be as easy as the Union cavalry general had thought. On the other hand, Sheridan made this observation to one of Grant's aides:

This force [Pickett's] is in more danger than I am in—if I am cut off from the Army of the Potomac, it is cut off from Lee's army, and not a man in it should ever be allowed to get back to Lee. We at last have drawn the enemy's infantry out of its fortification, and this is our chance to attack it.

Sheridan's losses at Dinwiddie Court House were 40 killed, 254 wounded and 60 missing. He wrote Grant that Pickett's force "is too strong for us. I will hold on to Dinwiddie Court-House until I am compelled to leave." Although Southern losses are not positively known, the best estimates are that the cavalry lost about 360 casualties out of 7,400 engaged, while the infantry lost 400 out of 3,100. Also, General Terry was no longer able to command his brigade, as he was hurt when a cannon shot struck his horse, causing it to fall with the general; Colonel Joseph Mayo, Jr., of the 3rd Virginia Infantry, assumed command.

Hold Five Forks At All Hazards!

South of White Oak Road and west of Claiborne Road, near the William Dabney house, Bartlett's brigade of the V Corps began its journey down a small wooded by-way in hopes of finding Sheridan. By dark the men reached the plantation of Dr. James P. Boisseau on Crump Road. There they went into position overlooking a branch of Gravelly Run, which put them in rear of Pickett's left flank. In the giant chess game of war, Pickett had earlier put Sheridan in check

George E. Pickett, CSA

at Dinwiddie Court House; now Warren's single brigade had placed Pickett's force in check.

At eight o'clock in the evening, General Meade ordered Warren to recall his troops and send one division to Sheridan at Dinwiddie Court House. Warren informed Meade that this would take some time, as the Boydton Plank Road bridge over Gravelly Run had been destroyed by the Confederates. At 10:30 the order was given for the movement: Ayres' division would move by the plank road to join with Sheridan's cavalry, while Crawford and Griffin marched via Bartlett's route.

Considerable time was lost by Ayres as his troops waited for the bridge to be reconstructed. Normally Gravelly Run could be forded by infantry without problem, but the heavy spring rains had overflowed its banks. It wasn't until two o'clock in the morning that the bridge was finally open for passage. Ayres joined Sheridan after daybreak and was dispatched to Turkey Egg Road. Warren personally went with Griffin and Crawford to Dr. Boisseau's on Crump Road where they arrived at about 7:00 a.m.

Pickett possibly did not know the exact size or location of Bartlett's brigade, but he did figure that Federal infantry was in his rear with probably more on the way, so he decided to withdraw to Five Forks. At 4:00 a.m. the Confederates began leaving their camps on the Adams plantation. Munford's cavalry covered the infantry's rear along Courthouse Road, while Rosser's and Rooney Lee's divisions recrossed Chamberlain's Bed to Scott's Road. While Pickett could boast of a tactical victory at Dinwiddie Court House, strategically he had gained nothing. During his ensuing retrograde movement Pickett received a fateful message from Robert E. Lee: "Hold Five Forks at all hazards." The commanding general further explained: "Protect road to Ford's Depot and prevent Union forces from striking the Southside Railroad.

Samuel W. Crawford, USA

Regret exceedingly your forced withdrawal, and your inability to hold the advantage you gained [at Dinwiddie Court House]." The future movements of Pickett's command would be governed by this explicit order.

Five Forks was the intersection of White Oak Road (running east and west), Scott's Road to the southwest, Ford's Road (also known as Church Road) to the north, and Courthouse Road to the southeast. Located six miles northwest of Dinwiddie, Five Forks was the key to covering Lee's last supply line, the South Side Railroad, only two and a half miles north of the Forks. A rural setting, the area was a mosaic of a few large plantations and small farmsteads, mainly the property of Widow Mary Elizabeth Gilliam (pronounced Gill-em), named "Burnt Quarter," and the farms of James and Benjamin Boisseau. To the east of the junction were the Bass (or William T. Barnes) and Robert Sydnor houses, the ruins of an old place referred to as the Chimneys, along with the little white frame meeting house called Gravelly Run Methodist Episcopal Church. The surrounding terrain was largely covered with tangled thickets and pine woods, which were cut by ravines and interspersed with bogs and an occasional clearing. Dotting the fields and woods were large granite outcroppings, described as looking like sleeping elephants.

When Pickett returned to White Oak Road at Five Forks he set his men to building log and dirt breastworks along the roadway. With him were Johnson's two brigades and Fitz Lee's cavalry, about 9,000-10,000 troops. Their line extended over a mile and three-quarters, with the left flank being refused by a "return," or angle (hereafter referred to as the Angle), about 150 yards long. Holding the left were Ransom's North Carolinians and Wallace's South Carolinians; next were Steuart's Virginians, and covering the forks were three pieces of artillery from Willie Pegram's battalion. West of the Forks were Terry's Virginians (under

"Burnt Quarter," a previously unpublished photograph taken shortly after the end of the war. Some of Custer's men, absent officers, visited the place and left calling cards, of sorts. They also stole a harp, damaged it, and later abandoned the instrument in a nearby woods, with a note identifying themselves as troopers from Capehart's brigade. (See also Pp. 156 & 157.)

Petersburg National Battlefield

Colonel Mayo), then Corse's Virginians, whose right was supported by three of Pegram's guns.

Guarding the right flank were cavalrymen under Rooney Lee, composed of General R. L. T. Beale's Virginians and General Rufus Barringer's North Carolinians. Rooney Lee's other brigade, under General William P. Roberts, covered the four mile gap between Pickett and Anderson at Claiborne Road. Munford's cavalry guarded the immediate Confederate left flank, which was also supported by four guns of Captain William M. McGregor's battery. The rest of Pickett's cavalry, Rosser's division, was sent about a mile and a half north of the Forks, across Hatcher's Run, to guard the wagons. Sizing up the situation, Pickett figured that the Federals would try to get between his force and Anderson's Corps to the east. Consequently, Pickett sent General Lee a telegram expressing his concerns and asking that a diversion be made to prevent him from being isolated at Five Forks. He also believed that Lee might send reinforcements.

As his men continued working on their entrenchments, George Pickett, along with Fitz Lee, received an invitation from Tom Rosser to join him for lunch at his camp a thousand feet north of Hatcher's Run. A few days earlier, while at the Nottoway River, Rosser had borrowed a seine and went dipping for shad (see Appendix 3). Generally a large-sized fish, it had to be specially baked (actually broiled) because it contained many small bones. Now that the Confederate army seemed to have a little respite from the fighting and marching it had seen over the last couple of days, the officers hoped to take time out for a shad-bake. Detecting no apparent movement by Sheridan to attack at Five Forks, it seemed relatively safe for Pickett and Fitz Lee to leave the front lines for awhile.

Meanwhile Custer's division had set out in immediate pursuit upon finding that the Confederates had deserted their camps north of Dinwiddie Court

Thomas L. Rosser, CSA

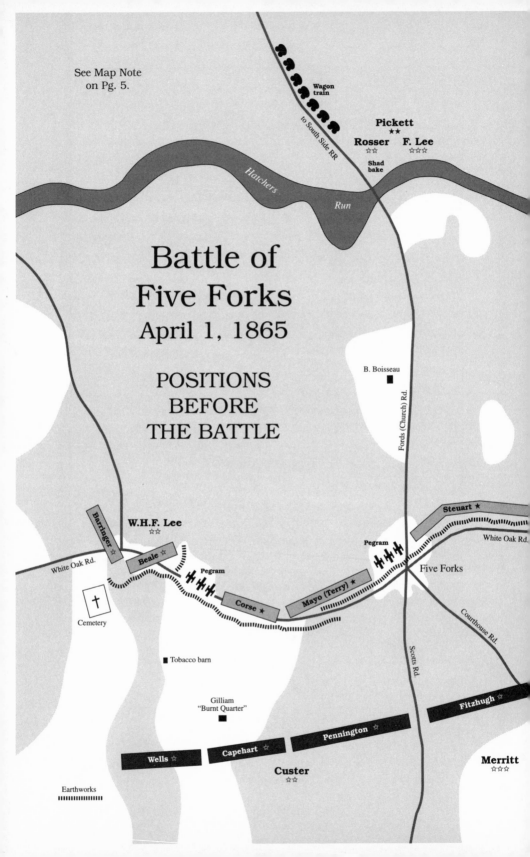

Battle of
Five Forks
April 1, 1865

POSITIONS
BEFORE
THE BATTLE

See Map Note
on Pg. 5.

Wagon train

to South Side RR

Pickett
★★
Rosser   F. Lee
☆☆   ☆☆☆

Shad bake

Hatchers
Run

B. Boisseau ■

Fords (Church) Rd.

Steuart ★

White Oak Rd.

Barringer
☆

W.H.F. Lee
☆☆

Pegram

Beale ☆

Pegram

White Oak Rd.

Corse ★

Mayo (Terry) ★

Five Forks

✝
Cemetery

Courthouse Rd.

Tobacco barn ■

Scots Rd.

Gilliam
"Burnt Quarter"
■

Fitzhugh ★

Pennington ☆

Wells ☆   Capehart ☆

Merritt
☆☆☆

Custer
☆☆

Earthworks
IIIIIIIIIIIIIIII

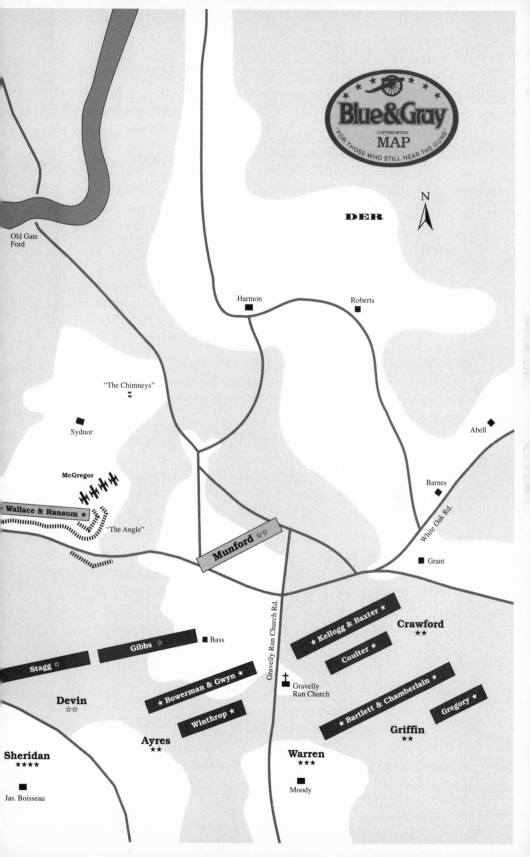

Blue&Gray
COPYRIGHTED
MAP
"FOR THOSE WHO STILL HEAR THE GUNS"

N

DER

Old Gate
Ford

Harmon ■

Roberts ■

"The Chimneys"
=

■ Sydnor

McGregor

Wallace & Ransom ★

"The Angle"

Munford ☆☆

Abell ◆

Barnes ■

White Oak Rd.

■ Grant

Kellogg & Baxter ★

Crawford
★★

Coulter

Gibbs ☆   ■ Bass

Stagg ☆

Bowerman & Gwyn ★

Winthrop ★

Gravelly Run Church Rd.

† Gravelly
Run Church

Bartlett & Chamberlain ★

Gregory ★

Griffin
★★

Devin
☆☆

Ayres
★★

Warren
★★★

Sheridan
★★★★

■ Jas. Boisseau

■ Moody

House on the morning of April 1. Shortly afterward he was followed by Devin, while Crook remained back at the village to guard the wagon trains and Little Five Forks (Gregg's brigade was assigned this duty), protecting Sheridan's left flank.

When Custer reached the junction of Courthouse and Turkey Egg roads, he found Ayres' infantry division coming into position. Moving toward the Confederate right flank along White Oak Road north of Burnt Quarter, Custer pushed his men cross-country through the woods toward Scott's Road. Devin, following on Courthouse Road, moved up to the fork where Crump Road led off and there encountered Griffin's division coming down from Dr. Boisseau's. Continuing his march, Devin eventually came upon Pickett's line at Five Forks. After feeling out the enemy's position, Devin aligned his troopers: Fitzhugh's brigade on the left as far as Scott's Road; Stagg extending east from Courthouse Road; Gibbs' men dismounted and guarding the extreme right near the Bass farm.

Custer's lead brigade, Pennington's, pushed across Scott's Road and encountered enemy pickets near Widow Gilliam's place. In the brief encounter that swirled around Burnt Quarter and into the peach orchard behind the house, the Federals were able to send the Southern cavalry back to their lines. Pennington then moved his troopers into position on Fitzhugh's left at Scott's Road. While awaiting the rest of the division the men built slight log breastworks.

On the morning of the 1st, Sheridan received reinforcements in the form of more cavalry from the Army of the James. Commanded by Ranald Mackenzie, the two small brigades really only amounted to the size of one good regiment. After resting his troops near Dinwiddie, Mackenzie was sent up Crump Road toward White Oak Road.

As Sheridan impatiently awaited the arrival of the remainder of Warren's forces, he received a dispatch

Commanding Warren's First Division was General Charles Griffin, the crusty looking fellow with the slouch hat in the center of the view. His staff poses with him, and the familiar Maltese Cross of the V Corps appears on the flag.

from his commanding general via a courier: "General Grant directs me to say to you, that if in your judgment the Fifth Corps would do better under one of the division commanders, you are authorized to relieve General Warren, and order him to report to General Grant, at headquarters." Sheridan's dislike for Warren was obviously shared by Grant. Warren's fate as a corps commander rested in the hands of "Little Phil" Sheridan.

Waiting for the infantry, Sheridan decided his battle plan for Five Forks. He would send Custer's division on a feint against the Confederate right, while the V Corps assaulted the Rebel left. The rest of the cavalry would press the Southern infantry in their front, attacking when the V Corps became actively engaged. Warren's men, assembled around the John Boisseau farm near the forks of Crump and Courthouse roads, received word about 1:00 p.m. to move forward. They marched a short distance and then veered off to the northeast up the Gravelly Run Church Road. Upon reaching some lowlands just south of the church their guide was instructed to "put the corps into position on this road obliquely to and at a point but a short distance from the White Oak Road and about one mile from the Five Forks."

Crawford led the line of march, followed by Griffin, then Ayres. It was close to 4:00 p.m. by the time Warren had his force of about 12,000 men (originally 15,000, minus losses over the previous three days) readied for the attack. Forming his battlelines in the bottom covering a 1000-yard front, Warren instructed his three division commanders to move forward *en echelon* until they struck White Oak Road. At that point, according to a sketch provided by Sheridan, they were to wheel to the left and smash into the Confederate flank at the Angle.

Ayres formed the left of Warren's line, Crawford the right, with Griffin in reserve. The two lead divisions were to assault in the "equivalent of three lines

The "Boy General," George Armstrong Custer, USA

of battle." Coinciding with this, Sheridan's troopers, numbering about 9,000-10,000 (although all would not be engaged), were to press the Southern line all along their front. Once Warren's troops began their forward movement, the V Corps commander instructed his divisions "to keep closed to the left and to preserve their direction in the woods, by keeping the sun, then shining brightly, in the same position over their left shoulders." It had taken close to three hours for Warren to move and ready his corps for the attack Sheridan had ordered. Little Phil grew even more impatient because of this perceived tardiness: "I was exceedingly anxious to attack at once, for the sun was getting low, and we had to fight or go back. It was no place to intrench, and it would have been shameful to have gone back with no result. . . ." Sheridan felt that Warren gave "the impression that he wished the sun to go down before the dispositions for the attack could be completed."

To the east of Warren's position, at the intersection of Crump and White Oak roads, Mackenzie's cavalry division was about to attack Roberts' North Carolina cavalry brigade. (At age 23, Roberts was the youngest general in the Confederate army. His adversary, General Mackenzie, was 24.) With Colonel Samuel P. Spear's 11th Pennsylvania Cavalry in the lead, Mackenzie's column fell upon the Southern horsemen, scattering them without much resistance as the North Carolinians either rode back to Pickett's force or over to Anderson's. In this short action, in which Colonel Spear was wounded, White Oak Road was cleared of any Confederate force from Claiborne Road to Warren's right at Gravelly Run Church Road. White Oak Road could no longer be used by General Lee to reinforce Pickett. After this success, Mackenzie rode westward to join Warren.

Back in Pickett's line, Fitz Lee was preparing to leave for the shad-bake. Munford rode up with a message that Roberts' brigade had been forced to give up its position when attacked by some Yankee cavalry, but Lee, either "impatiently hungry or uncritically skeptical," said: "Well, Munford, I wish you would go over in person at once and see what this means and, if necessary, order up your Division and let me hear from you." Fitz Lee then rode off to Rosser's camp, leaving Rooney Lee in charge of the cavalry at the front. Since Pickett had already left to have lunch at Rosser's, "Maryland" Steuart was in charge of the infantry. It appears that none of the Confederate officers on the front lines knew where the commanding generals had gone.

Due to a faulty map and poor reconnaissance work, the V Corps was under the impression that Pickett's left flank extended to the intersection of Gravelly Run Church Road and White Oak Road. When the advancing columns reached this point and began to wheel, they found that the Angle they were to assault was still three-quarters of a mile to the west. This caused the three columns to diverge somewhat from the original alignment. Leaving their position below the church at approximately 4:15 p.m., the Federals moved through the woods and fields bordering White Oak Road. Because of the necessary realignment, Ayres would now be hitting the Confederate left flank at the Angle. With Sheridan and Warren riding in front of the troops, Ayres readjusted some of his brigades. Colonel Richard N. Bowerman's Marylanders—Bowerman had taken command from the wounded Colonel Denison—and Gwyn's Pennsylvania and Delaware troops would now be supported by Winthrop's New York brigade.

Before reaching the Angle, Federal skirmishers ran into resistance from Munford's cavalry posted in front of Ransom. Munford, watching with increasing trepidation as the entire Yankee V Corps formed up across from him, repeatedly sent messages to Fitz

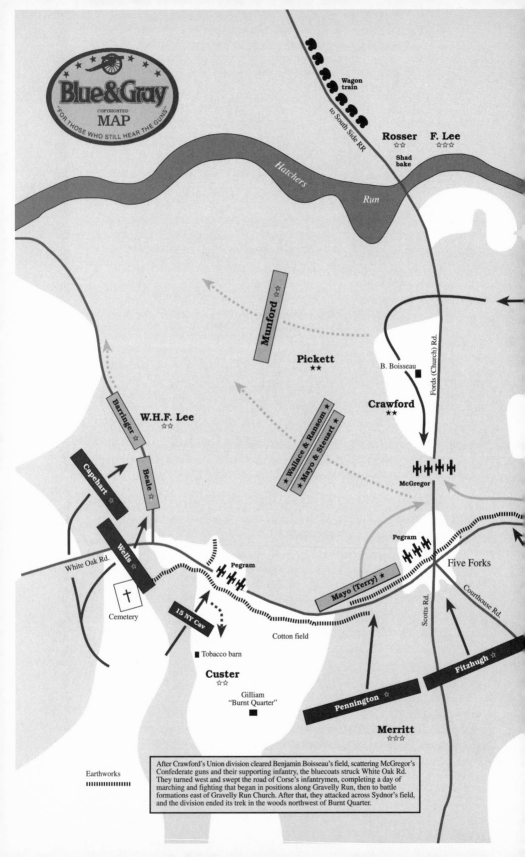

Blue & Gray
COPYRIGHTED
MAP
"FOR THOSE WHO STILL HEAR THE GUNS"

Wagon train

to South Side RR

Rosser ☆☆

F. Lee ☆☆☆

Shad bake

Hatchers

Run

Munford ☆

Pickett ★★

B. Boisseau ■

Fords (Church) Rd.

Crawford ★★

Barringer ☆

W.H.F. Lee ☆☆

★ Wallace & Ransom ★
★ Mayo & Steuart ★

McGregor

Capehart ☆

Beale ☆

Wells ☆

White Oak Rd.

Pegram

✝
Cemetery

15 NY Cav

Pegram

Pegram

Five Forks

Mayo (Terry) ★

Scotts Rd.

Courthouse Rd.

Cotton field

■ Tobacco barn

Custer ☆☆

Gilliam "Burnt Quarter" ■

Pennington ☆

Fitzhugh ☆

Merritt ☆☆☆

Earthworks
ıııııııııııı

After Crawford's Union division cleared Benjamin Boisseau's field, scattering McGregor's Confederate guns and their supporting infantry, the bluecoats struck White Oak Rd. They turned west and swept the road of Corse's infantrymen, completing a day of marching and fighting that began in positions along Gravelly Run, then to battle formations east of Gravelly Run Church. After that, they attacked across Sydnor's field, and the division ended its trek in the woods northwest of Burnt Quarter.

Lee and Pickett, but not one of the couriers could find them. Exasperated, Munford even asked Ransom for the use of McGregor's battery to fire on the gathering enemy, but the North Carolina general refused to allow this. Attempting to hold his own, behind some hastily built fence rail "pens," Munford's troopers eventually had to give way to the advancing Union infantry. While the V Corps continued its rush on the Confederate flank, Sheridan ordered Mackenzie to cover Warren's right flank as far as Hatcher's Run to the north.

The area to the east of the Angle which Ayres' men had to traverse was generally open, until they reached the woods in which the Angle was built. Behind and to the north of this Confederate entrenchment was a large open area, cut by deep ravines, known as Sydnor's field. Robert Sydnor's farmhouse was located in the middle of it, and northeast of his place were the house ruins known as the Chimneys. The Angle itself, because of the construction of traverses, was divided into small rooms, in order to protect the defenders from crossfire. Immediately behind the end of the work was a small lunette for one of McGregor's guns.

As Ayres' men moved forward to attack the Angle, Crawford's troops, having to cover more ground because his division was on the outward part of the wheel, lost contact with Ayres' right. This development caused Warren to ride away from the main column to attempt to bring Crawford's division back into the battle.

Meanwhile, as the Federals approached Ransom's position, Confederate fire caused some of Gywn's men to waver. Sheridan saw this and called out in his electrifying voice: "Go at 'em with a will! Move on at a clean jump or you'll not catch one of them. They're all getting ready to run now, and if you don't get them in five minutes, they'll every one get away from you! Now go for them!" Mounted on his black horse "Rienzi,"

Romeyn B. Ayres, USA

Sheridan grabbed his red and white swallow-tailed guidon and rode up and down the battleline encouraging the men to move forward. Since the Confederate entrenchment—the Angle—was only 150 yards in length, Gwyn's brigade, on Ayres' right, would actually overlap it.

As the Union infantry approached, in what must have appeared to be swarms, some of Ransom's men began to give ground. McGregor, realizing the inevitable, limbered his four pieces and rode off toward Ford's Road. He did so just as the first of the assaulting troops climbed the three-foot high works. A member of the 190th-191st Pennsylvania claimed to be the first to plant his unit's colors on the Angle. Those North Carolinians who did not retreat were either killed or captured in the Federal onslaught. The Confederate left flank quickly crumbled.

Riding up to the Angle, Sheridan jumped Rienzi over the wall and landed among a group of prisoners. They called out to him in a Southern drawl: "Whar do you want us-all to go to?" Pointing to Gravelly Run Church in the rear, he replied: "Get right along, now. Drop your guns; you'll never need them anymore. You'll all be safe over there. Are there any more of you? We want every one of you fellows." And the attackers bagged plenty of them.

The initial attack at the Angle rounded up about a thousand prisoners for the Federals, and numerous battleflags. But a cost was paid for them. Colonel Frederic Winthrop was mortally wounded, shot through the left lung, and Colonel Bowerman was severely injured—two out of Ayres' three brigade commanders.*

---

* Frederic Winthrop, a former bank clerk born in New York City, rose to Colonel of the 5th New York Veteran Infantry and eventually brigade command. He was breveted brigadier general in 1864, and as a result of his conspicuous bravery at Five Forks he would receive a posthumous brevet promotion to major general. Winthrop was buried in Brooklyn.

Frederic W. Winthrop, USA

Frederic Winthrop Family

With acknowledgment to Patrick A. Schroeder, author of *We Came to Fight:
The History of the 5th New York Veteran Volunteer Infantry, Duryee's Zouaves (1863-1865)*

While Ayres' men continued their mopping-up operation at the Angle, Devin's and Custer's troopers kept the rest of the Confederates occupied along their front. Meanwhile, Crawford was still swinging way too far to the north, across Sydnor's field, while Warren, along with several couriers sent by Sheridan, attempted to bring him back. Griffin's division was up, and fell in between Ayres and Crawford. By this time Ayres had reformed his division and was ordered to continue the advance down White Oak Road. Griffin, sensing something had gone wrong with the order of attack, rode up to Ayres to find out what had happened. "Nothing much," replied Ayres. "Nothing new. The same old story, Crawford [has] gone off and left me to fight alone."

Those Southerners who were not gobbled up in the initial attack fell back on Wallace's South Carolinians, whose left flank was now exposed. In turn, Wallace's troops and Ransom's remnants fell in on Steuart's left; Steuart's flank rested in some woods on the western edge of Sydnor's field. Some of Steuart's men, along with those of Wallace and Ransom, constructed another line of works along the edge of the woods perpendicular to the main line.

One of Crawford's brigades, under Colonel John A. Kellogg, managed to get separated from the rest of the division in its swing to the north. Warren happened upon them, told Kellogg to halt and stay where he was, then Warren rode off to find the rest of Crawford's command. Shortly, an orderly from Sheridan found Kellogg and added to the confusion by ordering him across Sydnor's field. Reaching the Sydnor house the infantrymen encountered some of Munford's cavalry posted in the building. Before he was able to rejoin Crawford, Kellogg had to bring up the 91st New York to dislodge the enemy skirmishers.

Behind Kellogg was Griffin's division, which was halted in the woods northeast of Sydnor's field. Here

George H. "Maryland" Steuart, CSA

Griffin received orders from Warren "to bring his division toward White Oak road, by the left flank." His three brigades, Gregory's, Chamberlain's and Bartlett's (the latter with only three regiments, the rest having wandered off with Crawford), moved forward, encountering Warren. Since Ayres had already taken the Angle, Warren ordered Griffin to push toward Ford's Road.

As Griffin moved across Sydnor's field, he became aware of Confederates posted along the edge of the woods on Steuart's left. Chamberlain's brigade (185th New York and 198th Pennsylvania), reinforced by the 188th New York, was the first to come in contact with the newly-entrenched Southern position. Passing through numerous ravines formed by wet-weather creeks, most of which emptied into Hatcher's Run, Chamberlain's infantry crashed into this enemy line. The 185th New York and a battalion of Pennsylvanians broke through and advanced toward White Oak Road. The other battalion of the 198th Pennsylvania and the 188th New York kept the rest of the Southern line occupied as Bartlett's three regiments—1st Michigan, 20th Maine and 155th Pennsylvania—came up. These three units ran into heavy resistance; the 155th Pennsylvania actually fought hand-to-hand with the Rebel defenders. Because of fierce enemy fire, some of Bartlett's men were forced to take cover behind the slight entrenchments.

Chamberlain heard of Bartlett's troubles and sent reinforcements. With heftier numbers the Federals surged ahead. This time the remnants of Ransom's and Wallace's commands, along with Steuart's Brigade, broke and fell back toward Ford's Road. Once again, Warren's infantry captured a large number of Confederate prisoners and numerous battleflags, including one from the 9th Virginia, which was taken by a member of the 20th Maine. Griffin's division continued pressing the remaining Confederates to Ford's

Joseph J. Bartlett, USA

Road, where Bartlett's men captured a train of ambulances. The Confederates were in dire straits and Pickett was nowhere in sight.

During the time that Ayres' and Griffin's divisions were rolling up the Confederate line from its left flank to Five Forks, Crawford's division continued its long, circuitous march north of the fighting. Passing across the upper edge of Sydnor's field and through heavily wooded and rolling terrain, cut by thickly overgrown ravines, the only action Crawford's men saw until reaching Ford's Road was in pushing back Munford's dismounted cavalry skirmishers. Upon reaching the road, the bluecoats captured seven ambulances and several wagons from Wallace's Brigade. The point that Crawford came onto the road was an open field at the farmhouse of Benjamin Boisseau. As Crawford moved his division into the open area, facing west, General Warren finally caught up with him. The corps commander ordered him to wheel his troops to the left, facing south, and to advance on the Confederate rear at Five Forks. As Crawford pressed forward as ordered, McGregor's four Rebel guns came in view astride the road facing him. Colonel Richard Coulter's brigade was ordered to attack the artillery position, and Coulter chose the 121st and 142nd Pennsylvania regiments for the purpose. The rest of his brigade formed on the right of the road in support, while Crawford's other two brigades (Kellogg's and General Henry Baxter's) massed *en echelon* on Coulter's right.

North of Hatcher's Run, the march by Crawford's division to reach Ford's Road did not go unnoticed by the Confederate generals at the shad-bake. Because most of the battlefield was heavily wooded, along with the fact that the dense pines were extremely damp from recent rains, Pickett and Fitz Lee did not hear much of the firing taking place along their left flank. Shortly after four in the afternoon, Pickett asked Rosser for a courier to carry a message to the front.

Fitzhugh Lee, CSA

The cavalry general, as was his habit, sent two—one in front of the other by a short distance, in the event trouble was encountered. As Rosser's two messengers forded Hatcher's Run at Ford's Road and headed for Five Forks, gunfire was heard and the lead courier was captured. The captors proved to be advance elements of Crawford's division.

Pickett witnessed the capture of Rosser's couriers. He leapt on his horse, splashed across the creek and immediately ran into the distraught Munford and his cavalrymen, who were trying to stem the Federal attack. The Confederate commander demanded of his cavalry officer: "What troops are these?" Munford told him that they were Fitz Lee's men, and he (Lee) of course was not there to take charge of them. Seeing more Union skirmishers coming through the woods, Pickett implored: "Do hold them back till I pass to Five Forks." In response, Captain James Breckinridge of the 2nd Virginia Cavalry charged with his troopers only to be shot and killed. But the short time bought by his brave act allowed Pickett to pass safely—riding forward on his horse, with his head away from the enemy to shield himself—and consequently was able to reach Five Forks. Fitz Lee also tried to rejoin his troopers at the front, but was unable to, because Crawford's men had spilled into the road. Instead Lee formed Rosser's division along the northern bank of Hatcher's Run to prevent the Federals from crossing and moving against the South Side Railroad.

When Pickett reached Five Forks he made an attempt to organize a line of resistance parallel to Ford's Road, using remnants of Steuart's, Wallace's and Ransom's shattered brigades. With the threat of Crawford now coming down in Pickett's rear, he pulled out most of Mayo's brigade and sent it to support McGregor's battery. Other Confederate stragglers rallied and joined this rear guard line. Once Munford's cavalrymen were pushed aside and Crawford deployed

Thomas T. Munford, CSA

his division, as ordered by Warren, Coulter's two assigned regiments moved against McGregor's Rebel artillery. As the Pennsylvanians reached the southern
edge of Boisseau's field, McGregor's four guns, protected by abatis, belched canister at the Yankees.
Coulter's regiments suffered heavily from this fire but
continued forward. Running into Mayo's Virginians,
the rest of Coulter's force was brought into action,
and along with the two support brigades bested the
Confederates, who either surrendered or fled southwest toward Gilliam's cotton field. Pickett ordered
Mayo to move cross-country to try to reach the South
Side Railroad as best he could.

Along with the Southern infantry taken by
Crawford, his men also captured three of McGregor's
guns. Warren then directed Crawford to oblique his
division to the right and push toward White Oak
Road. Warren's intention was to straddle the roadway west of Five Forks and cut that avenue of escape for Pickett's men. Marching in the same direction that Mayo had taken in reaching Gilliam's
field, the Federals had to pass through woods and
swamps before hitting White Oak Road. Their march
was directed by the sounds of battle coming from the
right flank, where Custer was tangling with Rooney
Lee's cavalry.

After the initial confrontation with Pennington's
lead regiments around Burnt Quarter, Rooney Lee's
two brigades went into position covering the Confederate right flank. As the rest of Pennington's blue troopers came on the field, they moved to the right and tried
to make contact with Devin's left at Scott's Road. Custer's
two remaining brigades, Colonels William Wells' and
Henry Capehart's, soon arrived and the "Boy General"
put them into position opposite Rooney Lee's force.
When the firing of the V Corps was heard against the
Angle on Pickett's left, Custer ordered an attack. To
cover this movement, Custer had the 15th New York

Henry Capehart, USA

Cavalry make a frontal attack on Corse's line, to keep Pegram's three guns of Captain Thomas Ellett's "Crenshaw" Battery occupied. These pieces were located between Corse's right and Lee's left. As the Union troopers charged the battery, Southern infantrymen poured a deadly fire into them. After two unsuccessful attempts to capture the guns, the New Yorkers fell back with heavy losses. While they were not successful in taking the guns, they did allow the rest of Custer's force to swing around on Rooney Lee's right flank. Trying to get around to the rear of the Confederate force, Custer's efforts were thwarted by Lee, who intercepted the flanking force. In fierce combat the Southern horsemen were able to prevent Custer from pushing forward to meet the V Corps, which was approaching from the east.

When Crawford reached White Oak Road he formed his battleline perpendicular to the road, facing west. By this time, with Mayo's (Terry's) brigade out of the way, Corse readied his brigade to meet the new Federal threat. Corse formed his men on the western edge of Gilliam's field, facing east, and built a light line of breastworks north of and at a right angle to the main line. Rooney Lee was backed up to this force, holding off Custer to the south and west. Crawford's troops were somewhat disorganized at this point, having been broken up in the movement through the woods from Ford's Road. General Warren, seeing that the men were not advancing against Corse's position at the edge of the cotton field, took matters into his own hands. It was near sunset as Warren personally took his corps flag in hand and called for his men to charge. When close to Corse's line, Warren's horse was shot from under him, but the attack was made. The encounter was brief as the Southerners either scattered or were taken prisoner. Again the Federals captured enemy battleflags, including the 32nd Virginia's, seized by a sergeant in the 11th Pennsylvania Infantry of Baxter's brigade.

William H. F. "Rooney" Lee, CSA

While Warren's men gathered in prisoners, Rooney Lee's cavalry joined Munford's troopers in riding out a woods road that led north across a branch of Hatcher's Run to Ford's Road. From that point they went to Church Road Crossing on the South Side Railroad, where the remnants of Pickett's force were gathering. Custer gave chase for a short distance, but darkness soon fell over the battlefield and he halted his pursuit. Back along Devin's and Pennington's front, the dismounted cavalrymen were also helping in the mop-up operation. Earlier, as the Confederate line collapsed during various stages of the battle, the Federal troopers did their part in keeping Southern infantry and artillery occupied. As the V Corps battleline (Ayres and Griffin) was approaching Five Forks, the Federal cavalry was charging enemy breastworks in their front.

Positioned at and west of Five Forks, the three guns of Willie Pegram's battalion opened fire with canister and shells from their 3-inch guns. One of the guns was from Captain Ellett's battery, the other two of Carpenter's (Alleghany Artillery) Battery, commanded by Lieutenant William Early. Willie Pegram's adjutant, Gordon McCabe, later wrote that he found this position "foolish," and "begged Pegram to protest against his posting 3 guns immediately at the junction of the roads, where they commanded nothing but the intervening road." While the highly skilled artillery commander probably agreed, he had his orders and did not disobey them.*

As Fitzhugh's brigade of Federal cavalry advanced in Pegram's front, and Union infantry closed on his left flank, Pegram told his cannoneers to fire their canister low. Mounted on horseback, young Pegram suddenly reeled as a bullet struck his left arm and

---

* Pegram's battalion fired Burton canister rounds and Read-Broun shells from their 3-inch guns. This information comes from written sources, confirmed by relics dug in the area.

William J. Pegram, CSA

side. Conveyed to a stretcher by McCabe, the bespec-
tacled 23-year-old colonel of artillery was borne from
the field and sent to Ford's Station on the railroad
where he died next day. Two months before, Willie's
brother, General John Pegram, had been killed along
Hatcher's Run, not eight miles from the spot where
the younger Pegram fell. Both were natives of Petersburg and died in its defense.

When McCabe returned after helping his wounded
commander from the field, he saw that the Federals
were overrunning the position at Five Forks. Lieutenant Early was killed at his guns, and a number of
cannoneers were wounded or captured. Two of the
guns were among the spoils for Fitzhugh's men,
though Pennington claimed to have captured them.
At the far northern edge of the battlefield, General
Mackenzie's small cavalry division swept back elements of Munford's skirmishers during Crawford's
movement to Ford's Road. At points during
Mackenzie's swing his men were actually forced to
cross Hatcher's Run to the north side, being squeezed
out by Crawford's line. Eventually they encountered
two V Corps regiments, the 118th Pennsylvania and
1st Maine Sharpshooters, who were assigned to guard
the crossing of Ford's Road at Hatcher's Run. Having
thus made contact with Warren's infantry, Mackenzie
was ordered to bivouac his troops in Benjamin
Boisseau's field.

The victory was complete for Sheridan's forces.
His combined infantry and cavalry had not only gained
the strategic road junction at Five Forks, but had scattered the defending enemy troops. The door was
wide open for the Union army to gain the South
Side Railroad. Grant received word of the breakthrough at Five Forks while at his headquarters, only
recently established near Dabney's sawmill, not far
from the battlefield. He went into his tent and wrote
out several orders that were sent over the telegraph

Ranald S. Mackenzie, USA

to all points along his Petersburg siege lines. One such fateful telegram read: "I have ordered an immediate assault along the lines." At daybreak on April 2, 1865, the VI Corps began the attack, and the end drew nearer for the Confederacy. One of Grant's officers recalled of that night (April 1-2) . . .

. . . all but the imperturbable general-in-chief were on their feet giving vent to wild demonstrations of joy. For some minutes there was a bewildering state of excitement, grasping of hands, tossing up of hats, and slapping of each other on the back. [The Battle of Five Forks] . . . meant the beginning of the end—the reaching of the "last ditch." It pointed to peace and home. Dignity was thrown to the winds.

A contemporary wrote that General Sheridan's victory at Five Forks had "no equal in the war for completeness and productiveness of great results. It opened the way for other successes, and it was the inauguration of a policy which crushed the rebellion within ten days."

On the other side of the battleline, word of the disaster soon reached Confederate army headquarters. At 5:45 that evening, General Anderson, whose corps was posted east of Five Forks, was ordered by Robert E. Lee to move immediately by way of Claiborne Road to the Church (or Ford's) Road Crossing on the South Side Railroad to reinforce Pickett. Hunton's Brigade led Anderson's column and actually arrived in time to connect with Rosser's Division along the north bank of Hatcher's Run, but Hunton's men did not become engaged in the fighting. With Stansel's (Moody's) and Wise's brigades following, the trenches along White Oak and Claiborne roads had to be filled with the brigades of McGowan and Joseph H. Hyman, both of Wilcox's Division, and William McRae and John R. Cooke of Heth's Division. To confront these new arrivals, Union General Humphreys of the II Corps sent Nelson Miles' division.

On the battlefield that night, the wounded were gathered up and taken to the field hospital set up at Gravelly Run Church. Earlier in the battle, one of the major casualties for the Federal army was carried there. Charles Wainwright recalled the scene as he passed through the large number of Confederate prisoners taken at the Angle, who were being sent to the rear:

They joked with our men along the line and I re-peatedly heard them say, "We are coming back into the Union, boys, we are coming back into the Union." *. . . But soon I saw that which was not joyful. In the very middle of these thousand prisoners, captured by his own brigade, came poor [Colonel Frederic] Winthrop; dead or at least very nearly dead, quite insensible and borne on the shoulders of four of his men. He had fallen just inside the rebel works, himself one of the first to cross them; he never spoke or [showed] any signs of consciousness.*

It was a glorious death to die, in the very moment of victory; a glorious funeral procession, the victor's body surrounded by the prisoners he had captured. But very sad to be shot down so young [25 years old], so beloved, so promising, just as the fight appears to be closing, and after having gone through four years of it unscathed.

Besides the loss of Colonel Winthrop, the Federal infantry could count 75 killed, 506 wounded and 53 missing, for a total of 634 casualties. Sheridan's cavalry lost 28 killed, 164 wounded and four missing, a total of 196, yielding combined Union casualties of 830. Exact Confederate casualties are unknown, but from the best sources it appears they had about 545 killed and wounded, and 2,000-2,400 captured. Although many sources list Pickett losing from 3,200 to 4,500 men as prisoners, a later compilation made from documents gathered for a Court of Inquiry shows that many counted in the inflated figures were troops not at Five Forks, but engaged elsewhere in the Petersburg lines.

On the morning of April 2, receiving orders from General Henry Heth, the four Confederate brigades placed in the White Oak Road and Claiborne Road trenches late on the 1st, withdrew from their fortified positions and headed up Claiborne Road to Sutherland Station. Shortly, Union General Miles, returning from an early-morning march to help Sheridan at Five Forks, began his pursuit of the enemy. As his lead brigade approached Sutherland Station around noon, the Federals made their first attack on the entrenched Confederate position parallel to the railroad. At 1:00 p.m. a second frontal attack was made as Miles brought up two brigades. Finally, between 3:30-4:00 p.m., with a third brigade attacking the enemy's left flank, Miles' force moved forward. The defenders could hold no longer, and the Confederates retreated from the field. The fighting at Sutherland Station on April 2nd proved to be the actual capturing of the South Side Railroad. Thus, Lee's final supply line into Petersburg was severed.

Pickett, cut off from the main Confederate army, escaped from the Five Forks battlefield with about 2,500 of his division and eventually joined forces with those of Bushrod Johnson. Both divisions constituted Anderson's Corps as they trudged on to Amelia Court House to be resupplied. Meanwhile, as Grant's stranglehold tightened at points along the Petersburg lines, Lee knew that April 1 would likely be his last night in the city. He telegraphed President Davis: "I think it is absolutely necessary that we should abandon our position. . . ." Under the cover of darkness on April 2, 1865, Robert E. Lee's troops sadly moved out of the "Cockade City," which they had so heroically defended for nine and a half months.

Confederate prisoners taken at Five Forks. The picture is worth thousands of words in describing the catastrophe that befell Lee's army on April 1, 1865.

Just after eight o'clock that evening, President Lincoln telegraphed Grant: "Allow me to tender to you, and all with you, the nation's grateful thanks for this additional, and magnificent success." Union troops occupied Richmond and Petersburg on the 3rd.

By April 5, Lee's whole army, including Pickett's weary division, was assembled at Amelia Court House awaiting supplies. Leaving that place hungry and disheartened when no supplies arrived, disaster once again befell Pickett's men in the Battle of Little Sailor's Creek, fought April 6. There he lost another 1,500 men in the last major engagement between the two great Eastern armies, a battle that cost the Confederates nearly a sixth of their force, mostly by capture. Relieved of his command by General Lee on April 8, Pickett, famous for his charge at Gettysburg, surrendered the remnants of his division—only 120 officers and 911 enlisted men—at Appomattox Court House the next day. When Lee saw Pickett, who evidently had not yet received the order relieving him, the commanding general remarked somewhat caustically: "I thought that man was no longer with the army."

In retrospect, the responsibility for the disaster at Five Forks certainly falls on Pickett's shoulders. The story of the shad-bake and its role in the battle did not come to light until many years later. Thomas Rosser, host of the shad-bake, wrote in 1902: "Pickett's conduct at Five Forks was the cause of Genl. R. E. Lee's losing all confidence in him, and had the opportunity been given, he would have been courtmartialed— He failed to guard his left flank, and he failed to rejoin his command when Col. T. T. Munford reported the enemy advancing." General Rosser also felt that Pickett and Fitz Lee took Munford's reports lightly. Rosser stated that "the position at Five Forks was considered so well chosen and strong, but little attention was given to [the] enemy's advance." (See Appendix 3.)

Pickett recorded in his official report that he "preferred the position behind Hatcher's Run" to that at Five Forks, as Hatcher's Run was where he had parked his wagons, and that he would have taken that position had he not received orders from Lee "to hold the road to Ford's." Pickett, obviously attempting to lay the blame elsewhere, added that he assumed Lee intended to send him reinforcements.

In what most would consider a joyous moment for both Sheridan and Warren, the latter was stunned by word received from his commander. Upon returning from the attack across Gilliam's field against Corse, Colonel George A. Forsyth rode up to Warren with a message: "Major-General Warren, commanding the Fifth Army Corps, is relieved from duty, and will report at once for orders to Lieutenant-General Grant, commanding Armies of the United States." Dazed, the infantry general rode to Sheridan and asked him to reconsider the action. The hot-tempered Irishman replied: "Reconsider? Hell! I don't reconsider my determination." Sheridan selected Charles Griffin to replace Warren as commander of the V Corps, with General Bartlett then assuming command of Griffin's division. Almost immediately, General Warren requested a Court of Inquiry to address the charges against him. Because of the rapidly following events that led to the closing of the war, combined with Grant's and Sheridan's political influence in the years after the war, Warren would not be granted his request until 1879. Generally speaking, Sheridan's "accusations or imputations" against Warren were:

1. In moving to gain White Oak Road on March 31, Warren moved with but one division rather than the entire corps, thus resulting in a repulse.

2. Warren did not move according to the expectations of Grant, thus allowing the enemy to escape from Dinwiddie Court House.

3. Warren did not urge his corps to get up fast enough on the 1st, acting as though "he wished the sun to go down before dispositions for the attack could be completed."

4. In the engagement at Five Forks, portions of Warren's line (Gwyn's brigade) gave way when not exposed to heavy fire, simply for want of confidence not given by Warren.

General Grant noted:

I was so much dissatisfied with Warren's dilatory movements in the Battle of White Oak Road, and in his failure to reach Sheridan in time, that I was very much afraid that in the last moment he would fail Sheridan. He was a man of fine intelligence, great earnestness, quick perception, and could make his dispositions as quickly as any officer, under difficulties where he was forced to act. But I had before discovered a defect which was beyond his control, that was very prejudicial to his usefulness in emergencies like the one before us. He could see every danger at a glance before he had encountered it. He would not only make preparations to meet the danger which might occur, but he would inform his commanding officers what others should do while he was executing his move.

This was not the first time Warren had gotten into trouble with his superiors. At the Battle of Spotsylvania Court House in May 1864, and later, in the June 18 assault on Petersburg, Warren came close to being relieved of command. At Five Forks, with the end so close in sight, it appears that Grant just did not want to take a chance with Warren.

Members of the V Corps felt strongly that their commander had been wronged at Five Forks. His artillery brigade commander, Charles S. Wainwright, wrote: "To me his removal at this time, and after the victory had been won, appears wrong and very cruel. It seems that even had he been removed just before, the victory should have covered up very big faults, and Sheridan should have restored him at once. . . ." When the Court of Inquiry convened in 1879, more than 1,700 pages of testimony from former officers in both Union and Confederate armies were taken. The final outcome on each of the charges was:

1. Exonerated, but Warren "should have been with his advanced divisions [in front of White Oak Road] and should have started earlier to the front."

2. It was not practicable for the V Corps to reach Sheridan by midnight on the 31st. "Warren should have moved Griffin and Crawford at once, as ordered."

3. It was found that there was no unnecessary delay in the march of the corps, and Warren had taken the usual methods of a commander to prevent a delay. Also, "his actions do not appear to have corresponded with such a wish" for the sun to go down, as was charged.

4. Warren was found to have exerted himself to remedy the situation (the divergence of Crawford and Griffin), and "this was for him the essential point to be attended to which also exacted his whole efforts to accomplish."

On November 21, 1882, the vindicating findings were published, and no other action was taken. Unfortunately, Gouverneur K. Warren—hero of Gettysburg, where his monument stands at the crest of Little Round Top, with bronze eyes gazing across the Valley of Death—had died a few months earlier, on August 8. It was said that the general "died of a broken heart." He was buried without a military funeral, in plain citizen's dress, as he had come to shun all the trappings of a soldier.

Rufus Barringer, CSA

WITH SHOUTS OF TRIUMPH AND TRUMPETS BLOWING

George Custer Versus Rufus Barringer at Namozine Church

April 3, 1865

by Chris Calkins

Historian, Petersburg National Battlefield, Virginia

Maps prepared by Dave Roth of
Blue & Gray Magazine

AS PHIL SHERIDAN'S BLUECLAD troopers broke camp at Widow Gilliam's plantation on the battlefield of Five Forks, the pungent smell of gunpowder still permeated the air. To them it was the smell of victory, knowing the evening before they had successfully smashed General George E. Pickett's force and gained access to the long-sought-after South Side Railroad. It was the 2nd of April, 1865, and off to the east the sound of gunfire could be heard distinctly at different points around Petersburg, Virginia. With Five Forks in his possession, Ulysses S. Grant ordered a series of assaults against Robert E. Lee's entrenched lines, knowing it was the right time to break the siege. The first such assault, led by General Horatio Wright's VI Corps, cut through the Confederate line southwest of Petersburg along the Boydton Plank Road. In the fight, Confederate General A. P. Hill rode forward hoping to stop the rout of his men, only to be confronted by two Federal soldiers; the result was the death of Lee's Third Corps commander. Coinciding with this attack, Union General John Parke's IX Corps moved from its position at Fort Sedgwick, astride the Jerusalem Plank Road, and assaulted the Confederate lines around Fort Mahone. While they would capture the initial line of works, stiff resistance kept them from making any farther advance throughout the day.

After the VI Corps broke through the line held by General Henry Heth's division, Wright's men pushed down the works all the way to the area of Burgess' Mill on Hatcher's Run, driving the Confederate defenders away. In support of this movement, both the

A. P. Hill, CSA

Army of the James, commanded by General Edward O. C. Ord, and General Andrew A. Humphreys' II Corps, Army of the Potomac, attacked Lee's lines south of the VI Corps' position. Consequently, Confederate troops holding the right flank were either forced to withdraw into the interior lines west of the city or be cut off from the main army. Those that already had been cut off moved to Sutherland Station on the South Side Railroad. There they would reform for the protection of that vital supply route.

As the VI Corps continued its sweeping action, Ord's army, composed of the XXIV Corps under General John Gibbon, and the XXV Corps made up entirely of United States Colored Troops, pushed up the Boydton Plank Road until they reached Lee's western outposts: Forts Whitworth and Gregg. At 1:00 p.m. Gibbon assaulted the position with his force of 5,000. The two forts were garrisoned by about 300 men who were told to hold at all costs. After withstanding three attacks they were finally overwhelmed by Gibbon's force and suffered great loss; however, this "Homeric Defense" allowed Lee to substantially man his inner line, located just west of the city boundary, to await another Federal attack.

As this eventful day (April 2) came to a close, the Confederates defending the railroad at Sutherland Station, about seven miles west of Petersburg, prepared for another Federal onslaught. General Nelson Miles of the II Corps came upon them as he moved his division up Claiborne Road. After making three attacks on the defenders, he forced them to scatter up the Namozine Road, relinquishing the rail line. Grant's final objective, the South Side Railroad, was now in Federal hands.

Back at the western environs of the city, with the sun now setting, Wright's VI Corps made one last attempt to get into Petersburg. They attacked Lee's inner line along Rohoic Creek at the Cox Road crossing.

As they pushed forward upon this position, General Lee was forced to give up his headquarters at the Turnbull house, called "Edge Hill," and move into the city. There he made arrangements for his army to withdraw that night, passing to the north side of the Appomattox River. The evacuation of Petersburg was now underway, as was that of Richmond. Darkness brought to an end the fighting of April 2, 1865.

While the Federal forces that brought victory at Five Forks the day before were not actively involved in the final assaults of April 2, they too were active this day. Sheridan ordered the V Corps, now commanded by General Charles Griffin (after General Warren's relief from command the night before), to move eastward down White Oak Road. Reaching the area of Claiborne Road and finding Miles' column of the II Corps advancing along it toward Sutherland Station, the V Corps returned to Five Forks and began moving up Ford's (or Church) Road. Running into resistance at Hatcher's Run, the corps eventually reached the South Side Railroad and the parallel Cox Road. After skirmishing with elements of Fitzhugh Lee's cavalry, they reached a point one mile west of Sutherland Station where they heard the final stages of Miles' fight. Turning north on a by-way, they came to Namozine Road, bivouacking at its intersection with the River Road.

Sheridan's cavalry followed the V Corps up Ford's Road, reaching the South Side at Crowder's Crossing (or Church Road Crossing), just south of Cox Road. At this point they came in contact with General Rooney Lee's cavalry, which quickly fell back. A running fight then ensued as the horsemen moved north along Ford's Road, past Ford's Meeting House. Eventually they came to Brown's Road at Trinity Church and continued northward to the intersection with Namozine Road at Scott's Cross Roads. As the advancing Federal troopers reached this area after a five-mile ride, they found the Confederates dug in along the ridge of Namozine Road. A halt was ordered until the division could regroup.

The remnants of Pickett's and Bushrod Johnson's divisions, which escaped from the debacle at Five Forks, eventually rendezvoused during the night in the Crowder's Crossing area. This point was half-way between Sutherland Station and Ford's Depot on the South Side Railroad. Early on the 2nd, after assembling the survivors, Pickett led off, followed by Johnson, both now under General Richard Anderson's command. The Confederate cavalry under Fitzhugh Lee brought up the rear, with Rooney Lee's division acting as rear guard. The column moved northward to Namozine Road, reaching it near its crossing of Namozine Creek at 3:00 p.m. About one and a half miles southeast of the creek, on high ground where Brown's Road intersected Namozine Road (Scott's Cross Roads or Corners), the men began erecting barricades. Fitzhugh Lee informed Johnson that Federal cavalry was pursuing him and would be on the scene shortly. Around 5:00 p.m. the bluecoats began arriving south of the intersection.

Pickett's men, being in the van of the column that left Crowder's Crossing, had continued up Brown's Road past Namozine Church in an attempt to cross the Appomattox River to the north side. They eventually reached the ferry at Exeter Mills that morning. The Appomattox was too deep to ford and too much time would be lost if an attempt to ferry the men across was made (but most of Ransom's brigade did get through). Pickett then decided to move his men farther about 15 miles where a bridge was located (probably Bevil's Bridge). He would march unmolested this day.

Sheridan's First Division, under General Thomas Devin, led the advance up Brown's Road and came in contact with Johnson's force at Scott's Cross Roads.

Colonel Charles Fitzhugh's Second Brigade of Devin's division prepared for an attack, with support by Colonel Peter Stagg's First Brigade (dismounted) and Captain Marcus Miller's horse artillery. General Alfred Gibbs' Reserve Brigade would remain mounted on the flank and in support of Miller's battery. The Federal horse soldiers made their first assault on the Rebel barricades about 6:30 p.m., but were repulsed by artillery and infantry fire. They would charge the position two more times, the last being about 8:00 p.m., with little results. Darkness now covered the battlefield and the troopers went into bivouac, but not before a connection was made with the V Corps, which was camped within a mile to the east along Namozine Road at the Williams' farm.

General Johnson remarked that his men suffered little or no loss in the three attacks by Devin. At 11:00 p.m. Johnson moved his column westward over the 50-foot-wide Namozine Creek, with General Eppa Hunton's brigade covering the passage. By 2:00 a.m. the Confederate army was safely across. While this was transpiring, at 1:00 a.m. Johnson received a dispatch from General Anderson, whose headquarters were up ahead at Namozine Church, concerning road conditions. Johnson was instructed to take Cousin's Road at the church and go to Bevil's Bridge via Cralle's (Crawley's) and Deep Creek roads. Later that morning these instructions were amended to follow the wagon trains into Amelia Court House, rather than going to Bevil's Bridge. As the column left the Namozine Creek crossing, the cavalry rearguard under General William P. Roberts began erecting earthworks along the western bank to contest any crossing by the Federals. Roberts' Brigade had the 4th and 16th North Carolina regiments along with a Virginia regiment as the crossing guards. It would be early morning before Sheridan's men appeared on the high ground overlooking the creek.

Since Devin's First Division had led the Federal column the day before and saw the brunt of the action at Scott's Cross Roads, on April 3 it was decided that General George A. Custer's Third Division would lead the chase. In the van was Colonel William Wells' brigade, composed of the 8th and 15th New York and 1st Vermont cavalry regiments. This force found Roberts' Confederate brigade posted at the Namozine Creek crossing, having destroyed the bridge over it. Bringing up an artillery piece from Lord's battery and loading it with canister, a dismounted cavalry force from the 1st Vermont crossed the creek under the gun's heavy covering fire. Passing upstream some distance they were able to flank Roberts' position and force him to retreat. Once this was accomplished, felled trees and other obstructions were removed from the road crossing point of the creek, and Custer's men forded without mishap. No major defensive stands were made by the Rebels for the next five miles or so, until Namozine Church was reached. To slow the progress of the advancing Federals, felled trees and piled fence rails were occasionally placed in the road. Along this route the cavalry found examples of the enemy's hasty retreat, such as artillery ammunition tossed away on the sides of the road and in the woods. The explosion of these shells could be heard as the Yankees rode by, the Southerners having set fire to fences and woods. Intermixed with the discarded shells were a number of disabled caissons and wagons, along with arms, accoutrements, blankets, clothing and cartridges. The 8th New York was leading the advance as Namozine Road approached Cousin's Road just east of the church.

The rear guard position of the Confederate column that morning was held by Rooney Lee's cavalry division, with Rufus Barringer's North Carolina brigade the rear-most unit, having changed places with Roberts. Barringer's small brigade was composed of

William P. Roberts, CSA

the 1st, 2nd and 5th North Carolina cavalry regiments (his 3rd North Carolina regiment was guarding the wagon train). After leaving the creek crossing, the Tarheels rode on a few miles to the summit of a hill near the church, which was reached about nine o'clock that morning (April 3). General Barringer, with the help of Generals Fitzhugh Lee and Rooney Lee, posted his regiments around the church, which sat at the intersection of Namozine, Cousin's and Green's roads. Holding his left flank was the 1st North Carolina, the center held by the 2nd, with the 5th dismounted on the right. One gun of McGregor's Battery was placed in position to the left of Green's Road. Less than 800 men made up the line. In front of the North Carolinians was an open field about 400 yards across, in the middle of which was the Abner Burke house. Beyond and east of the dwelling were woods, through which the enemy soon appeared as they trotted down Namozine Road.

As the 8th New York cleared the trees, the horsemen charged the Confederates at the church, driving the Rebel pickets back on their reserves before falling back themselves. The 1st Vermont now joined the 8th New York as both renewed the attack on Barringer's line, the 8th attempting to move on the left flank of the 1st North Carolina. Seeing this, General Barringer turned to his courier, Frank Brown, and said: "Order that . . . [Second] Regiment to charge and you lead it." This charge proved futile as the 1st North Carolina soon broke under the flank attack by the 8th New York. At this point orders were sent to the 5th North Carolina to retire from its position near the church and for the men to regain their horses. Barringer's withdrawal now became a stampede as more Federal troops entered the fight, namely the 15th New York. As the Confederates fled, McGregor poured his last shot into the blue troopers, while "raving like a mad man." General Barringer, seeing that the 5th

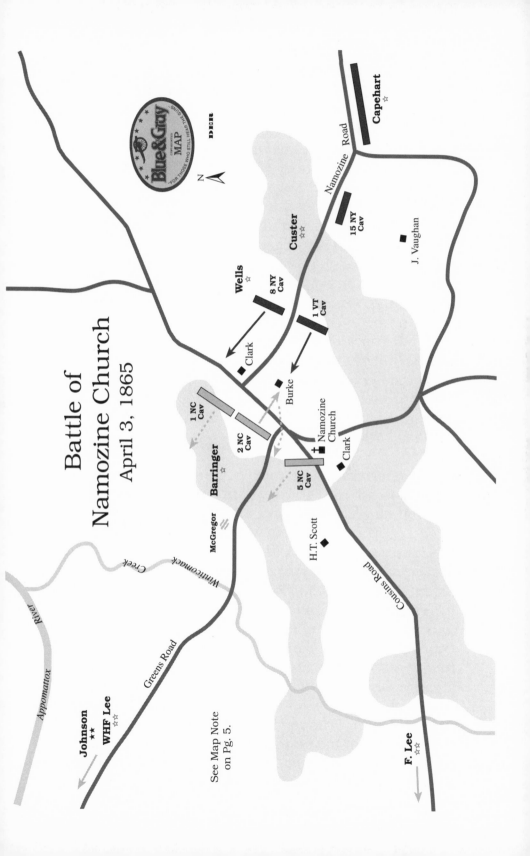

was not retiring as ordered, dashed across the field with two of his staff to guide the dismounted men, in person, through a heavy woods still unoccupied by the enemy. This act saved the troopers from capture, although their horses were lost. A soldier in the 8th New York, Oscar Palmer of Company B, remembered the running fight at Namozine Church:

They [the Confederates] were in a piece of woods and did not fire on us until we were very close. Since there were only a few of us on advance, we could not charge until more came up, so we took shelter behind an old log building. Among the rest was Capt. Goodrich who was shot there. The ball entered his forehead and came out on the back side of his head. . . . We took him back to the church where other wounded were being cared for. By the time we got force enough to make an effective charge they had slipped out, leaving some laying around there (dead and wounded) that they could not very well take.

As General Barringer's men fell back along Green's Road, the 8th New York continued the chase. Palmer remembered:

The next stand they made was on top of quite a hill. . . . Our regiment . . . formed in double line at the foot of the hill in a piece of woods. . . . Just over the hill was a heavy [enemy] skirmish line. . . . [Major James] Bliss was wild, he rode up to me and said: "give them hell." I gave them seven shots and reloaded my carbine. By that time some of the boys came and the Major ordered them to form in line for a saber charge. I dropped my carbine to my side, as usual, and for some reason it unsnapped and dropped to the ground. I dismounted and readjusted my carbine and remounted, but before I had straightened up in the saddle, was struck in the neck. . . . The Major . . . rode up to know how badly I

Postwar image of Oscar Palmer of Company B, 8th New York Cavalry. He was wounded at Namozine Church.

Petersburg National Battlefield

was hurt and if I thought I could get back to the church alone. [This was Namozine Church, which was about one mile from the battlefield.] I told him I thought I was shot somewhere in the shoulder. . . . The ball went into the top of my shoulder, just cutting the inside of my coat collar and coming out about three inches from where it went in, down on my back. I rode my horse back to Namozine Church, which was used as a hospital, stayed there until ambulance train came up. . . . Am now at Burkeville Station on the Danville Road. . . .

In the fight at Namozine Church, Wells' brigade captured 350 of Barringer's men, as well as 100 horses and McGregor's gun. Quartermaster Sergeant Jerome B. Hatch of the 1st Vermont claimed the honor for the capture of the gun. The cost was two killed and nine wounded in the 1st Vermont, one killed and six wounded in the 8th New York (Captain Asa Goodrich, mentioned above, would die of his wounds on April 30), and one killed in the 15th New York. No casualty figures are available for the North Carolinians. General Rufus Barringer remembered his role and subsequent capture in the battle:

I was ordered by Mjr. Gen. Lee to hold the position as long as I safely could. I stated the condition of my Brigade, its loss of officers and utter exhaustion, but there was no alternative. . . . Soon the enemy appeared in force, with shouts of triumph and trumpets blowing. . . . I ordered the whole [force] to fall back and skirmish in retreat. The 5th Regt, which was dismounted, fought with . . . obstinacy and seemed slow to give up the contest. Before it retired under further orders, the enemy had gained the main road of retreat. I then moved this reg. by marching through forests and byways, and conducted it safely out to a point six miles above, where I hoped to find Mjr. Gen. Lee and the rest of the Brigade. Nearing this point I found it

*picketted. While reconnoitering who the pickets were,
I was taken prisoner, with Lt. Foard, and three couriers, by a party of Sheridan's Scouts, dressed in Confederate uniform. The Reg't. learning of my capture,
made good its escape.*

At the same time, General Fitz Lee's adjutant general, Major J. Dugin Fergusson, was captured. Roger
Hannaford of the 2nd Ohio Cavalry in Colonel
Alexander Pennington's brigade recalled his coming
on the battlefield after the fight:

*At noon we came to a small church at a cross road &
here the advance of our Brig. [actually Division] came
on the rebel "rear guard" & charged them bringing in
many prisoners; some officers. A Capt [Goodrich] I think
of the 2d [8th] N.Y. Cav. lay in the little church, having
been shot thro' the head. He soon died. There were
some 3 or 4 men most of them badly wounded in the
church. We drew up in line thinking we might be called
on, after waiting an hour we again mounted, our Brig.
dividing the 3rd N.J. & 2nd N.Y. Cav, taking the left
hand road [actually the right, or Green's Road] while
our Regt & 1st Ct. took the left [Cousin's].*

General Bushrod Johnson's Confederate division
followed Green's Road this day along with Rooney Lee's
cavalry. Fitzhugh Lee's division, commanded by Thomas Munford, went down Cousin's Road to Cralle's
Road, then proceeded northward to the Deep Creek
bridge. Both contingents had to contend with crossing Winticomack Creek after leaving the Namozine
Church area. General Custer sent Wells' brigade after Fitz Lee while Colonel Henry Capehart's brigade
went after Rooney Lee. Colonel Pennington was ordered to send regiments in support of both Wells and
Capehart, keeping a reserve at the Namozine Church
crossroads. By 1:00 p.m. the Federal advance reached

Deep Creek on the road to Bevil's Bridge (Green's Road). In addition to the numerous prisoners taken along the route, the flag of the 2nd North Carolina Cavalry was captured. It was taken by General Custer's brother, Thomas, of the 6th Michigan Cavalry, who was given the Medal of Honor for the deed.

General Philip Sheridan reported from Namozine Church at 4:10 p.m. that "up to this hour we have taken about 1,200 prisoners, mostly of A. P. Hill's corps, and all accounts report the woods filled with deserters and stragglers, principally of this corps." General Wesley Merritt, riding with the column that went up Green's Road, informed Sheridan about the immediate situation from his headquarters at Dr. Taylor's, south of Deep Creek. Obtaining information from some locals it appeared that the Confederates were heading east toward Bevil's Bridge to cross the Appomattox. Merritt suggested that the cavalry move the next day on Amelia Court House.

After marching along Green's Road for a couple of miles, Bushrod Johnson received orders from General Anderson to take the next left-hand by-way and proceed back to Namozine Road (or Cousin's) with his column. The reason: it was learned that the bridge over Deep Creek was impassable at the Green's Road crossing. Upon reaching Namozine Road after a two mile march, and brushing aside some Federal pickets, Johnson was joined by Fitz Lee's cavalry. They continued the march to the fork with Cralle's Road near Mannboro where again the Yankees were met. Johnson sent out three of his brigades—Moody's, Wallace's and Wise's—who dispersed the Federals after a "sharp brush" in the area of Sweathouse Creek. The Southerners moved on and crossed Deep Creek at Brown's Bridge, going about five miles past Tabernacle Church to the vicinity of Bevil's Bridge Road. At this point Pickett's Division was found.

It was Custer's Third Brigade (Capehart's) supported by the 3rd New Jersey and 2nd New York that fought at Sweathouse Creek. The latter two units lost four killed and 24 wounded in the evening's engagement. In reporting the fight, Custer remarked, "Here a desperate struggle took place, which gave a temporary check to our further advance." That night his men went into camp along the creek.

As darkness came upon the Amelia County countryside, Merritt and his force camped in the area of Dr. Taylor's, between Green's and Cralle's roads. The house itself was used as a temporary hospital for some of the wounded from the fight at nearby Sweathouse Creek. The Confederate casualties were cared for at Mrs. Mann's, who was described by one of the wounded as "a very kind hearted lady she is kind to all." General Sheridan made his headquarters at Mrs. Cousin's, west of Namozine Church. The vanguard of the Federal infantry, Griffin's V Corps, went into camp near the crossing of Deep Creek.

The next day, April 4, Merritt, with Devin's division, continued the pursuit after crossing Deep Creek and pressed the enemy beyond Tabernacle Church to Beaverpond Creek and Drummond's Mill. The 1st Michigan was ordered to reconnoiter toward Bevil's Bridge while the division crossed the creek, and immediately ran into Heth's, Pickett's and Johnson's infantry forces covering the road to Amelia. Stagg's Wolverine brigade and part of Colonel Charles Fitzhugh's brigade began skirmishing with the Rebels in a fight that lasted until ten o'clock that evening. After burning the mill and seeing that Lee's army was concentrating on Amelia Court House, the cavalrymen returned to the main column and proceeded to ride west toward Jetersville Station on the Richmond & Danville Railroad. Figuring Lee would follow the railroad upon leaving Amelia Court House, this would be the logical point to intercept his column by setting a roadblock across his path. No major fighting would take place on the April 4, as the Confederates congregated at Amelia and the Federals maneuvered into position at Jetersville.

Back at Namozine Church, Yankee surgeons busily treated the wounded all through the night of the 3rd until ambulances could move them to the hospital at Wilson's Station on the South Side Railroad. After April 6 this establishment would be moved to Burke's Station at the junction of the South Side and Richmond & Danville railroads. The men wounded early in the battle at Namozine Church were taken into the church, with possibly some of Barringer's casualties sharing the building. Presumably those wounded around Sweathouse Creek eventually were brought to the church also.

Today Namozine Presbyterian Church is a small, rural, frame edifice measuring 24 by 35 feet, with a plainly furnished interior. Built in 1847, it has a seating capacity of 75, including an L-shaped gallery once used by slaves who accompanied their owners to services. The exterior is covered with beaded board siding. Louvered shutters, attached by hand-forged strap hinges, offer protection from the sun. Attesting to its use as a Civil War hospital, there are purported to be blood stains on the middle flooring. Presently this Amelia County church sits silently in a pine grove along Route 708, the old Namozine Road. A Virginia historical marker in the yard recalls the church's role in history: "LEE's RETREAT—Near Here Custer, Commanding Advance Guard of an Army of the Potomac, Struck and Drove Back Fitz Lee, Left Flank Guard of Army of Northern Virginia, April 3, 1865."

Sadly, in 1988, because of a dwindling congregation, the church was forced to close its doors after 140 years of service. As a kind, final gesture, the members provided the meeting house with a stabilizing facelift before turning it over to the Amelia County

Historical Society. The building is now in the hands of those who cherish their past, when the great armies of Lee and Grant passed through on the way to peace and unity at Appomattox Court House, six days after the clash at Namozine Church. The site is currently a stop on the renowned driving tour, "Lee's Retreat," where the story of the battle is provided via radio transmitter. Information on this driving tour can be obtained by calling 1-800-6-RETREAT.

ABOUT THE AUTHOR

CHRIS CALKINS, formerly serving as a Park Historian at Petersburg National Battlefield, was at the time of this publication Chief of Interpretation at the battlefield. Author of numerous publications, he helped write and design Virginia's "Lee's Retreat" driving tour, a model now used by many states and organizations. He is a native of Detroit, Michigan, graduated from Longwood University in Farmville, Virginia, and is married to the former Miss Sarah Brown of Appomattox. They live in a restored 18th century mansion in Petersburg's Old Towne Historic District.

MAPS were prepared by Dave Roth of *Blue & Gray Magazine*. They were drawn based on material supplied by the author.

AUTHOR'S SOURCES: Bearss, Edwin C. and Chris Calkins, *Battle of Five Forks*; Chamberlain, Joshua L., *The Passing of the Armies*; Freeman, Douglas Southall, *Lee's Lieutenants*, Vol. III, and *R.E. Lee: A Biography*; Harrison, Walter, *Pickett's Men: A Fragment of War History*; Humphreys, Andrew A., *The Virginia Campaign of '64 and '65*; Nevins, Allan, ed., *A Diary of Battle: Personal Journals of Colonel Charles S. Wainwright, 1861-65*; Newhall, Frederic C., *With General Sheridan in Lee's Last Campaign*; Papers of the Military Historical Society of Massachusetts, "The Shenandoah Campaigns of 1862 and 1864" and "The Appomattox Campaign 1865," Vol. VI; Paulette, Sam, "Retreat from Petersburg to Sailor's Creek," *The Farmville Herald*; Porter, Horace, *Campaigning with Grant*; Powell, William H., *The Fifth Army Corps*; Suderow, Bryce A., *Confederate Strengths & Losses from March 25-April 9, 1865*, and *Union Casualties in the Appomattox Campaign*; Tremain, Henry Edwin, *Last Hours of Sheridan's Cavalry*. Also consulted were the *Official Records* and *Atlas*, *Battles and Leaders*, Vol. IV, and numerous secondary sources.

PHOTOS and other illustrations, unless otherwise indicated, are courtesy of Library of Congress, National Archives, USAMHI, Petersburg National Battlefield, and other public holdings.

ACKNOWLEDGED for valuable cooperation and assistance in the preparation of this work are: Chris Calkins and his lovely wife, Sarah; Superintendent Frank J. Deckert, John Davis, James Blankenship, Jr., and Ray Brown, of Petersburg National Battlefield, Va.; Bryce A. Suderow for permission to quote from his statistical documents; Dewey Cashwell, Dinwiddie County Administrator; Leonard Ponder, Dinwiddie County Planner; Mr. William Bolte, former Commissioner of Revenue, Dinwiddie County; and area property owners Mr. & Mrs. Stephen Perry, James H. Ritchie and Dan Robbins. Also the Frederic Winthrop Family, with acknowledgment to Patrick A. Schroeder, author of *We Came to Fight: The History of the 5th New York Veteran Volunteer Infantry, Duryee's Zouaves (1863-1865)*; and Eastern National, Fort Washington, Pa., and its representative, Rachel Shumsky, who materially assisted with bringing Chris Calkins' work back into print with this publication. B&G Tour Assistant was E. Chris Evans.

THE General's TOUR

The Battle of Five Forks

Including the Battles of Lewis' Farm, White Oak Road, and Dinwiddie Court House

With Supplemental Driving Tours of the Battle of Hatcher's Run and the Fight at Namozine Church

by Chris Calkins

Historian, Petersburg National Battlefield, Virginia

and Dave Roth

Editor, *Blue & Gray Magazine*

Maps prepared by Dave Roth

ANY TOUR OF EVENTS related to the Siege of Petersburg should begin at the Petersburg National Battlefield. The Visitor Center is located east of the town of Petersburg, Virginia, between I-95 and I-295, with other access off of US 301 & 460. The program and exhibits at the Visitor Center will help place the events of March 29 - April 2, 1865, within the context of the overall siege and spring campaign. (Refer to the Tour Map on Pp. 136-137.)

To begin your Tour of Five Forks, and the smaller engagements of Lewis' Farm, White Oak Road, and Dinwiddie Court House, leading up to the major battle, take the Dinwiddie Court House exit off of I-85 southwest of Petersburg, then proceed east on Rt. 703, Carson Road, in the opposite direction from the signpost for the Five Forks Unit of Petersburg National Battlefield. (Naturally the Blue & Gray Tour takes in considerably more than the National Park Service holdings, and our Tour brings you in to Five Forks by way of the Union V Corps' march, not necessarily the most direct route.) Proceed to the intersection with Old Vaughan Road and turn left. Then, in a short distance, just past Hunnicut Road, pause (if traffic permits) at the next intersection, before turning left onto Quaker Road. This is Blue & Gray's Tour Stop #1.

#1—VAUGHAN ROAD-QUAKER ROAD
INTERSECTION

Refer to the Maps on Pp. 37 & 39.

Coming down Vaughan Road (toward you) on March 29, 1865 was General G. K. Warren's V Corps, Army of the Potomac. The column turned north onto Quaker Road at this intersection. You should do the same, following Warren's route to the Lewis' Farm battlefield.

About a mile and a half up Quaker Road you will cross Gravelly Run, and it was here that Warren's troops first made contact with elements of Richard Anderson's corps of Lee's army. Pushing aside minor resistance at the crossing, Warren proceeded north and soon encountered stiffer competition at the Lewis Farm. The farm is located about three-quarters of a mile past where you cross over I-85. The ruins of the Lewis farmhouse are located in the field east of Quaker Road, but most of the heavy fighting took place in the field west of the road. The sawdust piles, a prominent feature of the battlefield, were located about a tenth of a mile north of the house and on the west side of the road. Pull over if you wish, exercising caution, and remember that the property is privately owned. This is our Tour Stop #2.

#2—THE BATTLE OF LEWIS' FARM
(or QUAKER ROAD)

Refer to the Maps on Pp. 37 & 39.

In the fight of March 29, Warren's corps was successful in gaining Robert E. Lee's wagon supply route into Petersburg, the Boydton Plank Road. Thanks to the efforts of Kenneth Discorfano, an admirer of General Chamberlain, a state historical marker was purchased and is now in place on the battlefield. It reads: "Quaker Road Engagement, 29 March, 1865. This was the first in a series of attempts by Grant's army to cut Lee's final supply line—the South Side Railroad—in the spring of 1865. Here at the Lewis Farm, Union forces

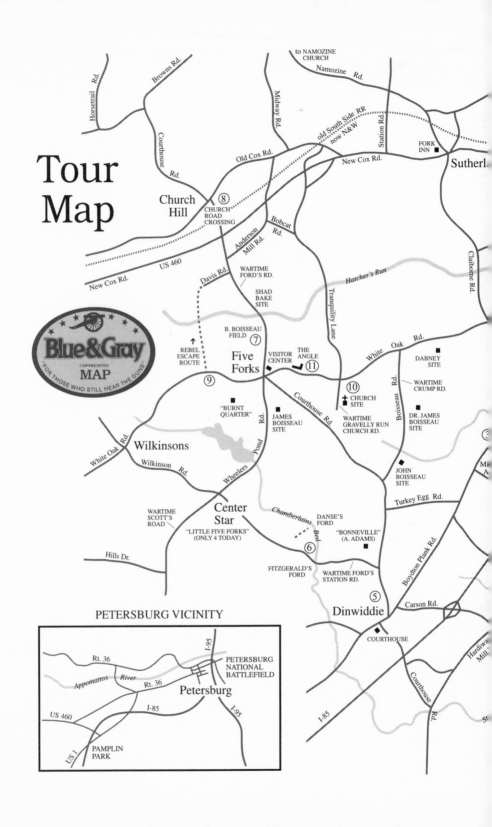

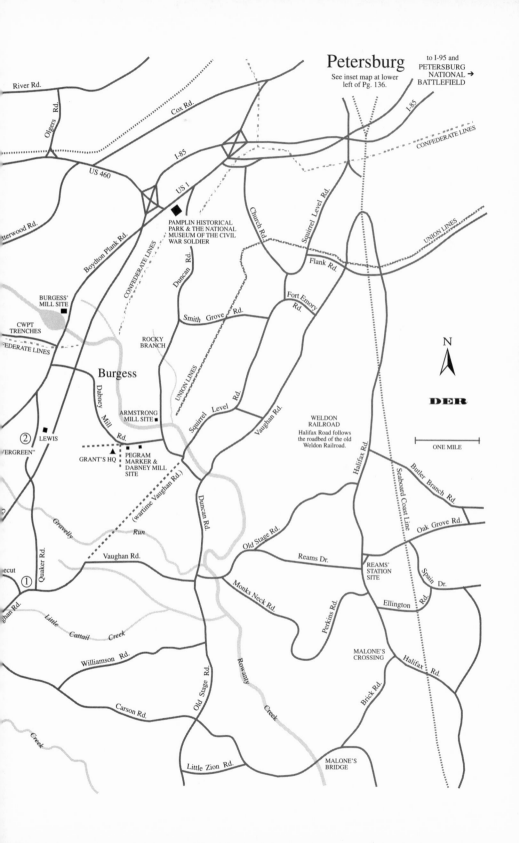

Petersburg
See inset map at lower
left of Pg. 136.

to I-95 and
PETERSBURG
NATIONAL →
BATTLEFIELD

River Rd.

Olgers Rd.

Cox Rd.

I-85

CONFEDERATE LINES

US 460

I-85

US 1

tterwood Rd.

Boydton Plank Rd.

PAMPLIN HISTORICAL
PARK & THE NATIONAL
MUSEUM OF THE CIVIL
WAR SOLDIER

Duncan Rd.

Church Rd.

Squirrel Level Rd.

UNION LINES

Flank Rd.

CONFEDERATE LINES

BURGESS'
MILL SITE

CWPT
TRENCHES

EDERATE LINES

Smith Grove Rd.

ROCKY
BRANCH

Fort Emory Rd.

Burgess

Dabney Mill Rd.

ARMSTRONG
MILL SITE

② LEWIS

ERGREEN"

GRANT'S HQ

PEGRAM
MARKER &
DABNEY MILL
SITE

UNION LINES

Squirrel Level Rd.

Vaughan Rd.

WELDON
RAILROAD
Halifax Road follows
the roadbed of the old
Weldon Railroad.

N

DER

ONE MILE

Halifax Rd.

Butler Branch Rd.

Seaboard Coast Line

Oak Grove Rd.

(wartime Vaughan Rd.)

Duncan Rd.

Run

Gravelly

Quaker Rd.

①

ecut

Vaughan Rd.

Old Stage Rd.

Reams Dr.

REAMS'
STATION
SITE

Spain Dr.

han Rd.

Little Cattail Creek

Williamson Rd.

Monks Neck Rd.

Perkins Rd.

Ellington Rd.

MALONE'S
CROSSING

Halifax Rd.

Carson Rd.

Old Stage Rd.

Rowanty Creek

Brick Rd.

Creek

Little Zion Rd.

MALONE'S
BRIDGE

led by Brig. Gen. Joshua L. Chamberlain engaged Confederates under Maj. Gen. Bushrod R. Johnson. After sharp fighting, the Union troops entrenched along nearby Boydton Plank Road and Johnson withdrew to his lines by White Oak Road. The Union Army cut the rail line four days later, after capturing Five Forks on 1 April."

Continue north on Quaker Road to the intersection with the Boydton Plank Road (US 1) and turn left. Precisely 1.0 mile from the turn you can see "Evergreen," the Butler house (or Wilson house on some period maps) on the left (east) side of the road, which served as Warren's headquarters. The house is privately owned and not open to the public. Proceed past the house to the crossing of Gravelly Run (see Pg. 140). We have now succeeded in placing you at a slight disadvantage, because in order to stop and read about the next tour stop, #3, you will have to cautiously locate a safe place to pull over near the crossing, and when you are finished exploring the area, you will have to make a U-turn to head back the way you came. Or, as we recommend, proceed beyond the Gravelly Run crossing a little farther down the road, where you will find more convenient and safe turn-around places. (If you are driving a big camper or some other over-sized vehicle, you might want to forego this stop.)

#3—BOYDTON PLANK ROAD CROSSING OF GRAVELLY RUN

The Boydton Plank Road was the principal route to Dinwiddie Court House. After the Battles of Lewis' Farm and White Oak Road, Warren was ordered to join General Philip Sheridan at Dinwiddie Court House. To do so, Warren first had to cross Gravelly Run, which at the time was 40 feet wide, due to recent rains—hard to believe as you gaze at the trickle

"Evergreen," near Gravelly Run, served as General Warren's head-quarters after the Battle of Lewis' Farm.

The Boydton Plank Road crossing of Gravelly Run. Heavy rains necessitated the construction of a 40-ft. bridge here, a task that slowed Warren's march to join Sheridan at Dinwiddie Court House. In the background is the creek's flood plain. The view is from the south bank.

that is Gravelly Run today. Notice the low ground east of the road. It is Gravelly Run's flood plain, and with a little imagination you can get an idea of how the small stream might gain greater proportions by spilling into this low ground. In order to join Sheridan, men of General Romeyn Ayres' division had to build a bridge, which was not completed until 2:00 a.m. on April 1 (refer to the opening paragraph on Pg. 30). Warren's delay in joining Sheridan at Dinwiddie Court House was one of the charges brought against the V Corps commander, who was dismissed after the Battle of Five Forks. Thus, this crossing point was a significant landmark in the career of General G. K. Warren.

Execute your turn-around and proceed north on the Boydton Plank Road (US 1) to White Oak Road, Rt. 613, and turn left. About three-quarters of a mile along White Oak Road turn right into the pull-over area provided on the near side of the White Oak Road-Claiborne Road intersection. The 75 acres of battlefield here, which include Confederate trenches from the Battle of White Oak Road, are currently owned and administered by the Civil War Preservation Trust, Inc. The organization is working closely with the Dinwiddie County Parks and Recreation Department, and has established an interpretive walking trail with waysides along the Confederate lines. This is our Tour Stop #4.

#4—BATTLE OF WHITE OAK ROAD
(or GRAVELLY RUN)

Refer to the Maps on Pp. 43 & 47.

The Confederate trenches here were part of General Richard H. Anderson's lines. Most of the fighting was off to the southwest, across White Oak Road, in the fields visible from the Southerners' position. A state historical marker is to be erected at this site, sponsored by the Dinwiddie County Confederate Memorial Association. Proposed wording: "White Oak Road Engagement, 31 March 1865. Union forces belonging to the V Corps, under Maj. Gen. Gouverneur K. Warren, sought to seize White Oak Road and sever the Confederate line of communication with Maj. Gen. George E. Pickett's detachment near Five Forks, four miles west. From here Gen. Robert E. Lee personally supervised the counterattack to Gravelly Run by Lt. Gen. Richard H. Anderson's corps. After a brief success, the Confederates were forced back into these entrenchments as Warren's men gained the important roadway."

Continue west along White Oak Road to Rt. 661, Boisseau Road (wartime Crump Road), and turn left. This intersection is where William Roberts' Confederate horsemen were scattered by Ranald Mackenzie's troopers during the opening phase of the Battle of Five Forks. Mackenzie was then able to ride west along White Oak Road to join Warren's attack at the Angle. Drive south on Boisseau Road, then bear left onto Courthouse Road, Rt. 627, and proceed to a right turn onto US 1, the Boydton Plank Road, which takes you into downtown Dinwiddie Court House. The leg of the trip along Courthouse Road follows the advance of Pickett's force during Phases III and IV of the Battle of Dinwiddie Court House (see the Maps on Pp. 61 & 65). Pull over and park at the courthouse, a landmark you can not miss.

#5—DINWIDDIE COURT HOUSE

Refer to the Maps on Pp. 57, 59, 61 & 65.

The present courthouse was built in 1851 and has seen several additions and alterations, such as the front columns. A marker on the lawn commemorates

Dinwiddie Court House. Except for the addition of columns on the front, the structure appears much the way it did to Yankee cavalrymen when they arrived on March 30, 1865.

Calvary Episcopal Church at Dinwiddie Court House was used as a hospital by the 1st Maine Cavalry after the Five Forks Campaign.

all the battles fought in the county during the war. Nearby is Calvary Episcopal Church, which was used by the 1st Maine Cavalry as a hospital during the Five Forks Campaign. After the war the building served as an office for the Freedmen's Bureau and for the Provost Marshal. In 1903 a claim was filed with the United States Court of Claims for damage inflicted by Federal troops. The money received was used to renovate the church to its present appearance. A small marker in the front yard was placed by the Dinwiddie Civil War Centennial Commission in memory of ten unknown Union soldiers, casualties of the Battle of Dinwiddie Court House, who were buried in the churchyard. Dinwiddie Court House was temporary headquarters for General Sheridan during operations against Five Forks. Another item of interest: One of the town's native sons was the venerable General Winfield Scott.

Leave Dinwiddie Court House by retracing your route on US 1 and Courthouse Road, the same roads you used to reach town. After a short distance on Courthouse Road, turn left onto Wilkinson Road, Rt. 611 (wartime Ford's Road). You will pass on your right the estate called "Bonneville," formerly the Adams house. While driving along Wilkinson Road you are going against the grain of Smith's Union brigade of cavalry as it fell back under pressure from Tom Rosser's and Rooney Lee's horsemen on March 31. In a short distance—just over a mile from your turn off of Courthouse Road—you will come to the swampy crossing of Chamberlain's Bed (see Pg. 147). Cautiously pull to the side of the road, and beware of soft ground. This is the Blue & Gray Stop #6.

#6—CHAMBERLAIN'S BED

Refer to the Maps on Pp. 57, 59, 61 & 65.

A tributary of Stony Creek, Chamberlain's Bed is here crossed at Fitzgerald's Ford, though a modern bridge makes passage much easier now than in 1865. Fitz Lee's cavalry forced a crossing here on March 31, but only after heavy fighting. Bluecoats of Colonel Charles Smith's brigade (Crook's division) held tenaciously on the high ground on the east bank. Among Smith's regiments was the 1st Maine

Blue & Gray Magazine Collection

Charles H. Smith, USA

Cavalry (the unit that used the Calvary Episcopal Church in Dinwiddie Court House as a hospital). The charge of Fitz Lee's troopers here at Chamberlain's Bed was described in the 1st Maine's regimental history: "That column of charging cavalry was a sight worth living to see. On they came, brave fellows, turning into the field a short distance from the creek, and still charging onward, and for a moment it seemed as if a hand-to-hand fight—mounted rebels against dismounted boys in blue—was inevitable. But the repeaters in the hands of the brave boys from Maine were too much for them. On they came, but came no nearer. Men and horses went down, and the head of the column remained in nearly the same place."

During the ensuing stand-off, the two sides glaring at one another across Chamberlain's Bed, a battle of the bands took place. The 1st Maine players struck up "Yankee Doodle," which a Rebel band answered with "Dixie." Another Union song was countered with "Bonnie Blue Flag," and "till late in the afternoon the two bands kept up a musical duel," the Maine historian penned, "inspiring the men of their respective sides with their martial

Fitzgerald's Ford on Chamberlain's Bed. The view is looking east along Wilkinson Road (wartime Ford's Station Road) toward the position held by Colonel Charles H. Smith's stubborn horsemen in blue.

strains. . . ." Later that afternoon, Smith's troopers fell back on Courthouse Road, joining Custer's division in a final line astride the road, a short distance north of Dinwiddie Court House.

Continue along Rt. 611 to its intersection with Rt. 645 at a place called "Little Five Forks" during the war, but only four roads meet here today. Turn right onto Rt. 645, called Wheeler's Pond Road, or Scott's Road at the time of the Civil War. Take Wheeler's Pond Road north to Five Forks, our Tour Stop #7. Pull into the small Visitor Center parking area.

#7—FIVE FORKS and the SHAD-BAKE

Refer to the Maps on Pp. 74-75 and 82-83.

Robert E. Lee told George Pickett, "Hold Five Forks at all hazards." Pickett failed him—miserably. The story is told of Pickett's postwar visit with Lee. After the meeting, as Pickett left with a companion, Pickett remarked caustically that Lee was the man who destroyed his division, a reference to Pickett's Charge at Gettysburg. Had Lee been similarly inclined to blame others, he might have charged that Pickett was the man who destroyed his army. Indeed, Pickett was one of the few officers of the Army of Northern Virginia for whom Lee came close to demonstrating outward dislike. You are standing at the quiet, country crossroads that on April 1, 1865, became the most important road junction in the existence of Lee's army, perhaps the whole Confederacy.

The evolution of Five Forks from the private to the public domain began in August 1962, when Congress authorized the addition of up to 1,200 acres at Five Forks to Petersburg National Battlefield. Funding was not sufficient, and for the next 30 years the Five Forks battleground remained in private

The Visitor Center at Five Forks. The view is looking north from the "V" formed by Wheeler's Pond Road (wartime Scott's Road) on the right, and White Oak Road on the left.

1—Burnt Quarter
2—Five Forks
3—The Angle
4—Ben Boisseau's Field
5—Sydnor's Field
6—Hatcher's Run
7—Shad Bake site

Photo: Petersburg National
Battlefield

hands. Then, in October 1989, the Richard King Mellon Foundation of Pittsburgh, Pennsylvania, in conjunction with The Conservation Fund, purchased 1,115 acres and obtained scenic easements on another 435 acres. The property was donated to the National Park Service in March 1991, and officially became the Five Forks Unit of Petersburg National Battlefield. Currently a 5-stop driving tour has been developed which explains the sequence of the battle. Information can be obtained at the Five Forks Unit Visitor Center.

After you have explored the historic crossroads of Five Forks, proceed north on Courthouse Road, Rt. 627, which passes to the left of the Visitor Center. A half-mile up this road, on the left side, is the site of Benjamin Boisseau's field, where Crawford's division charged McGregor's guns and Mayo's infantrymen. You will soon cross Hatcher's Run. Rosser's camp, scene of the fateful shad-bake, was located a thousand feet north of the creek, probably near the road, the exact location lost to history. Continue north to the little community of Church Hill, where Courthouse Road, also known as Church Road, or Ford's Road, strikes the tracks of the N & W Railroad. In 1865 this was known as the Church Road Crossing (see Pg. 154) of the South Side Railroad. Carefully pull over near the railroad crossing. This is our Tour Stop #8.

#8—SOUTH SIDE RAILROAD

Today the tracks belong to the N & W Railroad, but in 1865 this was known as the South Side Railroad, Lee's last supply artery running into the besieged city of Petersburg. Pickett's and Johnson's men reassembled here at Church Road Crossing after the Battle of Five Forks. The South Side was the target of Sheridan's offensive, although the Yankee army first got astride

Hatcher's Run where it is crossed by Courthouse Road (wartime Ford's Station Road). The view is looking west toward a large swampy area prominently shown on maps of the area. A thousand feet north of this spot, likely at a location near the road, is the shadbake site. (See Appendix 3.)

Church Road Crossing on the old South Side (now N&W) Railroad. Here the Confederates regrouped after their disaster at Five Forks. Federal troops reached Sutherland Station, four miles to the east, on April 2nd, severing Lee's lifeline once and for all. Fittingly, the train in the photograph is hauling into Petersburg. The view is looking north.

the railroad a little farther east, at Sutherland Station, on April 2.

Turn around and head back down Courthouse Road to Five Forks. At the Forks, take an odometer reading, then turn right onto White Oak Road and drive precisely 1.0 mile to a road trace leading north. Carefully pull to the side of the road.

#9—GILLIAM'S FIELD, BURNT QUARTER and the REBEL ESCAPE ROUTE

Refer to the Maps on Pp. 74-75 and 82-83.

South of White Oak Road is Gilliam's field, scene of the clash between Custer's cavalry and Rooney Lee's troopers. Also, it was here that Crawford' s division, of Warren's corps, struck White Oak Road, turned west, arrived in the area of Gilliam's field and attacked Corse's Confederates. (Crawford had launched an attack from the Gravelly Run Church area, making a wide swing to the north, across Sydnor's field, then a southerly attack down Courthouse Road through Benjamin Boisseau's field, to reach White Oak Road.) The Gilliam mansion (see Pg. 156), called "Burnt Quarter" (which is PRIVATE PROPERTY), bore witness to the fighting in the surrounding fields, and suffered some damage at the hands of Custer's troopers. Family portraits had faces slashed from the canvas with sabre blades, and contents of drawers were dumped onto the floor. Valuable furniture was treated with little regard. After the Yankee horsemen left, the Gilliams glued the faces back onto the paintings the best they could. The patched portraits still adorn the walls of Burnt Quarter today (see Pg. 157), the vandalism readily apparent. The trace leading north from where you have pulled over was the avenue of escape for most of the Rebels along this part of the Five Forks line.

"Burnt Quarter," the Gilliam estate (which remains in private hands, so do not trespass). Six unidentified Confederates killed in the Battle of Five Forks are buried in the yard. Compare this photograph to the wartime image on Pg. 71.

Dave Roth of Blue & Gray

Interior view of "Burnt Quarter" showing one of the
Gilliam family's patched portraits, which were damaged
by Custer's errant troopers.

Turn around, proceed back through Five Forks and stay on White Oak Road until making a right turn onto Tranquility Lane, wartime Gravelly Run Church Road. When the road dead-ends, make a U-turn and stop. This is our Tour Stop #10.

#10—SITE of GRAVELLY RUN METHODIST EPISCOPAL CHURCH

Refer to the Maps on Pp. 74-75 and 82-83.

The road past the church originally connected with Courthouse Road to the south, but is now blocked at the dead-end. Now that you have turned around and are facing north up Tranquility Lane, the church site is on your right. South of the church, Warren's three divisions formed for their assault on Pickett's left flank at Five Forks. Gravelly Run Methodist Episcopal Church, a 40-ft. by 36-ft. white frame structure, built in 1854, served as a field hospital after the battle. In 1906 the congregation filed a claim against the Federal government for destruction attributed to Union troops, which included: all the windows and doors had been taken and the pulpit destroyed; pews had been used for firewood, and floors were "all stained up with blood." The $800 asked for was to cover these damages plus provide compensation for the time the structure was used as a hospital. In the mid-1920s, with a diminished congregation, the church was abandoned and later sold for lumber. A nearby residence was constructed from it.

Proceed back to White Oak Road and turn left. Just under a mile from the turn, where White Oak Road makes a slight bend to the left, remains of the Confederate "angle" can still be located in the woods on the right side of the road, which is our Tour Stop #11. As of publication date, yellow tags attached to tree limbs alongside the road help locate the site. Carefully pull over in this vicinity. The earthworks are owned by the National Park Service, but easy access has not yet been provided. (If pressed for time, or if you are not properly equipped to tramp through brambles and woods, and mud, depending on the weather, you may want to forego this stop.)

#11—THE ANGLE

Refer to the Maps on Pp. 74-75 and 82-83.

The 150-yard-long "return," or the Angle in the Confederate line, was held by General Matthew W. Ransom's North Carolina infantry. You can still locate the "rooms," which were formed by traverses, where Ransom's men unsuccessfully attempted to stem the tide of Warren's attack. Among the first to leap into the captured works was General Sheridan himself.

Blue & Gray Magazine Collection

Matthew W. Ransom, CSA

Continue west on White Oak Road to Five Forks, where you can right onto Courthouse Road to reach US 460, or left onto Courthouse Road and proceed south to Dinwiddie Court House and connections to I-85. This concludes the main Blue & Gray Magazine Driving Tour. Supplemental Tours are on the following pages. Before leaving the area you might want to visit some sites not on the Tour, but marked on the Tour Map:

REAMS STATION SITE, *about 8 miles east of Dinwiddie Court House, along Halifax Road (the old*

Weldon Railroad bed): Point on the march of Sheridan's cavalry on their way to Five Forks; also scene of several actions during the war, principally the battle of August 25, 1864, between A. P. Hill's Confederate corps and Hancock's II Corps.

GRANT'S HEADQUARTERS, *about a mile southwest of Burgess on Dabney Mill Road*: This important historic site has no marker whatsoever. It was here that Ulysses S. Grant established temporary headquarters and soon received word of Sheridan's success at Five Forks. Grant issued orders for a general assault all along the lines for the next day—orders that resulted in the end of the war a week later. (This site is included on the Supplemental Driving Tour of the Battle of Hatcher's Run.)

END OF FIVE FORKS TOUR

SUPPLEMENTAL DRIVING TOUR

THE FIGHT AT NAMOZINE CHURCH
April 3, 1865

Refer to the Map on Pg. 123.

The intersection of US 460 and Rt. 708 northeast of Five Forks marks the location of Sutherland Station on the old South Side Railroad, Lee's last line of supply. A pullover on Rt. 708 near the tracks provides historical interpretation. Located here is the Fendall C. Sutherland house and tavern known as Fork Inn, built in 1803. After the Battle of Five Forks on April 1, 1865, and the Union Breakthrough of Lee's lines on April 2, the South Side was cut here at Sutherland Station by Union forces after a sharp fight.

Fork Inn at Sutherland Station

Dave Roth of Blue & Gray

Dave Roth of Blue & Gray

Namozine Church

Continue north then west on Rt. 708 into Amelia County and soon you will arrive at Namozine Church, a wartime structure.

Here on April 3, a cavalry clash occurred when elements of Union General George A. Custer's division struck Lee's rear guard composed of General Fitzhugh Lee's horsemen. In the fight, Confederate General Rufus Barringer was captured. Earlier that day, the church had served as headquarters for Confederate General Richard H. Anderson, commanding an infantry corps. After the fight, it was a hospital and headquarters for Union General Phil Sheridan.

You can backtrack along Rt. 708 to return to US 460, or you can reach that same highway by proceeding south on Rts. 611 or 627.

END OF NAMOZINE CHURCH TOUR

THE BATTLE OF HATCHER'S RUN
February 5-7, 1865

Refer to the Maps on Pp. 15, 17 & 21.

An excellent place to begin a Driving Tour of the Battle of Hatcher's Run is Pamplin Historical Park & The National Museum of the Civil War Soldier, located at 6125 Boydton Plank Road (US 1) southwest of Petersburg; take Exit 63-A off I-85 and proceed to the park entrance on US 1-South. The 422-acre park, situated on ground where the Union Breakthrough of Lee's lines occurred on April 2, 1865, was made possible by a $24 million gift from the Pamplin family. The park is owned and managed by the Pamplin Foundation, a private, nonprofit organization dedicated to historic preservation and public education.

Simulated earthworks at Pamplin Historical Park

Dave Roth of Blue & Gray

The National Museum of the Civil War Soldier

National Museum of the Civil War Soldier

The 25,000-sq.-ft. National Museum of the Civil War Soldier combines state-of-the-art technology and some 1,000 artifacts to tell the story of the common soldier from training camp to battle.

After touring the park, proceed south on Duncan Road, Rt. 670, approximately three miles to the crossing of Rocky Branch.

On your right is the Clements farm, bordering Rocky Branch, which is a small tributary of Hatcher's Run. As of publication date the Civil War Preservation Trust had acquired this tract, including the nineteenth century farmhouse. When fully developed, access will be provided to the main Confederate line at Hatcher's Run (a continuation of the lines running through Pamplin Historical Park). In this area numerous battles were fought along the Petersburg front, particularly the February 5, 1865, action in the three-day Battle of Hatcher's Run. Fighting had also occurred in this area on October 27, 1864, and would again on March 25 and April 2, 1865.

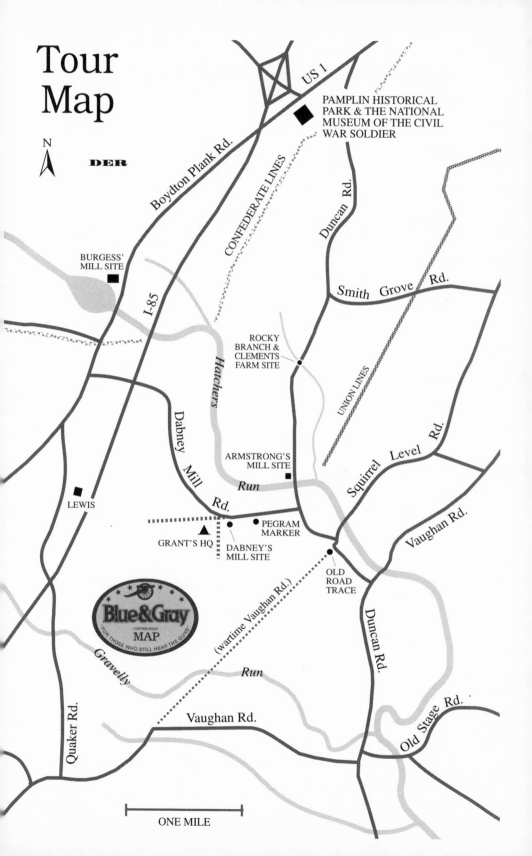

Continue south down Rt. 670 one mile to Hatcher's Run, where on your right you can see the site of Armstrong's Mill, the current structure being known as Steere's Mill. The millpond is postwar. Cross over Hatcher's Run and proceed to the end of Duncan Road (about three-quarters of a mile) until you reach Vaughan Road, Rt. 613, and turn right. In a short distance the road will make a dog-leg to the left while a dirt lane continues forward. This is the original Vaughan Road trace which played a prominent role in the military movements around Hatcher's Run and Gravelly Run. It is a private dead-end road, so turn around and retrace your route back toward Armstrong's Mill via Rt. 670. Proceed to Dabney Mill Road, Rt. 613, and turn left. Go a half-mile and look for a state historical marker on your left, then turn into the parking lot.

The parcel is owned by the Civil War Preservation Trust and is the site of the February 6 & 7 fighting at Hatcher's Run. Interpretive waysides with battle maps are provided, along with a small marker to Confederate General John Pegram, who fell on this field.

Pegram memorial

Dave Roth of Blue & Gray

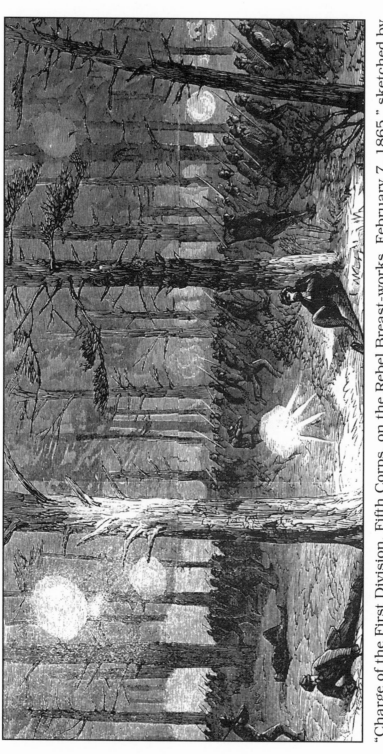

"Charge of the First Division, Fifth Corps, on the Rebel Breast-works, February 7, 1865," sketched by A. W. Warren. It appeared in the February 25, 1865 *Harper's Weekly.*

Petersburg National Battlefield

Leave the parking area by turning left. Located a short distance down the road where Rt. 613 bears to the right is the site of Dabney's Steam Sawmill (on your left).

At the time of the Battle of Hatcher's Run, Dabney's portable steam-operated sawmill had come and gone, and only its sawdust pile remained as a landmark on the battlefield. The site also played an important role on March 29, 1865, when General Grant and his staff moved their headquarters here from City Point as the scene of operations moved west of Petersburg. It was here that Grant heard of Sheridan's victory at Five Forks on April 1, and ordered an all-out assault on the Confederate lines early on the 2nd.

Continue along Dabney Mill Road until you reach the Boydton Plank Road, US 1, and turn right. This road follows the old turnpike that served as a supply artery for Lee's army, particularly after the Battle of Weldon Railroad (August 1864), which resulted in that rail line being cut by the Federals. As you drive north you will pass through the battlefield of Burgess' Mill (also known as the Battle of Boydton Plank Road or Hatcher's Run) fought October 27, 1864. At White Oak Road, Rt. 613, you can turn left to reach Five Forks, or follow US 1 to return to Pamplin Historical Park and Petersburg National Battlefield.

END OF HATCHER'S RUN TOUR

APPENDIX 1 — ORDER OF BATTLE

HATCHER'S RUN, February 5-7, 1865

UNION ARMY

II CORPS - MG Andrew A. Humphreys

Second Division - BG Thomas A. Smyth

First Brigade - COL William A. Olmstead
19th Maine   19th Massachusetts   20th Massachusetts
7th Michigan   1st Minnesota (two companies)
59th New York   152nd New York
184th Pennsylvania   36th Wisconsin

Second Brigade - COL Mathew Murphy (mortally wounded 2/5);
COL James P. McIvor
8th New York Heavy Artillery   155th New York
164th New York   170th New York   182nd New York

Third Brigade - LT COL Francis E. Pierce
14th Connecticut   1st Delaware   12th New Jersey
10th New York (battalion)   108th New York
4th Ohio (4 companies)   69th Pennsylvania
106th Pennsylvania (3 companies)
7th West Virginia (4 companies)

Third Division - Bvt. MG Gershom Mott

First Brigade - BG Regis De Trobriand
20th Indiana 1st Maine Heavy Artillery
17th Maine   40th New York   73rd New York
86th New York   124th New York   99th Pennsylvania
110th Pennsylvania   2nd U.S. Sharpshooters

Second Brigade - Bvt. BG George W. West
1st Massachusetts Heavy Artillery   5th Michigan
93rd New York   57th Pennsylvania
105th Pennsylvania   141st Pennsylvania

Third Brigade - Bvt. BG Robert McAllister
11th Massachusetts   7th New Jersey
8th New Jersey   11th New Jersey   120th New York

Artillery: Bvt. LT COL John G. Hazard
10th Massachusetts Lt. Artillery
4th U.S., Battery K

V CORPS - MG Gouverneur K. Warren

First Division - Bvt. MG Charles Griffin

First Brigade - Bvt. BG Horatio G. Sickel (wounded 2/6)
185th New York   198th Pennsylvania

Second Brigade - COL Allen L. Burr
187th New York (battalion)   188th New York (battalion)
189th New York

Third Brigade - Bvt. BG Alfred L. Pearson
20th Maine   32nd Massachusetts   1st Michigan
16th Michigan   83rd Pennsylvania (6 companies)
91st Pennsylvania   118th Pennsylvania   155th Pennsylvania

Second Division - Bvt. MG Romeyn B. Ayres

First Brigade - Bvt. BG Frederick Winthrop
5th New York   15th New York Heavy Artillery
140th New York   146th New York

Second Brigade - COL Richard N. Bowerman
1st Maryland   4th Maryland
7th Maryland   8th Maryland

Third Brigade - Bvt. BG James Gwyn
3rd Delaware   4th Delaware
157th Pennsylvania (4 companies)   190th Pennsylvania
191st Pennsylvania   210th Pennsylvania

Third Division - Bvt. MG Samuel W. Crawford

First Brigade - BG Edward Bragg
24th Michigan   143rd Pennsylvania   149th Pennsylvania
150th Pennsylvania   6th Wisconsin   7th Wisconsin

Second Brigade - BG Henry Baxter
16th Maine   39th Massachusetts   97th New York
11th Pennsylvania   88th Pennsylvania

Third Brigade - Bvt. BG Henry A. Morrow
94th New York   95th New York   147th New York
56th Pennsylvania   107th Pennsylvania
121st Pennsylvania   142nd Pennsylvania

Artillery - MAJ Robert H. Fitzhugh
9th Massachusetts Lt. Artillery
1st New York Lt. Artillery, Battery D
1st New York Lt. Artillery, Battery L

VI CORPS

First Division - Bvt. MG Frank Wheaton

First Brigade - LT COL Edward L. Campbell
1st New Jersey (3 companies)   2nd New Jersey (one company)
3rd New Jersey (one company)   4th New Jersey
10th New Jersey   15th New Jersey   40th New Jersey

Second Brigade - COL James Hubbard
2nd Connecticut Heavy Artillery   65th New York
121st New York   95th Pennsylvania

Third Brigade - Bvt. BG Joseph E. Hamblin
37th Massachusetts   49th Pennsylvania
82nd Pennsylvania   119th Pennsylvania
2nd Rhode Island (6 companies)   5th Wisconsin

IX CORPS

Third Division - BG John F. Hartranft

First Brigade - COL Charles W. Diven
200th Pennsylvania   208th Pennsylvania
209th Pennsylvania

Second Brigade - COL Joseph A. Mathews
205th Pennsylvania   207th Pennsylvania
211th Pennsylvania

CAVALRY - Bvt. MG David McM. Gregg

First Brigade - BG Henry E. Davies, Jr. (wounded 2/6)
1st Massachusetts   1st New Jersey   10th New York
24th New York   1st Pennsylvania (5 companies)
2nd U.S. Artillery, Battery A

Second Brigade - Bvt. BG J. Irvin Gregg (wounded 2/6);
COL Michael Kerwin
2nd Pennsylvania   4th Pennsylvania   8th Pennsylvania
13th Pennsylvania   16th Pennsylvania
1st U.S. Artillery, Batteries H & I

Third Brigade - COL Oliver B. Knowles
1st Maine   2nd New York Mounted Rifles
6th Ohio   13th Ohio
21st Pennsylvania

CONFEDERATE ARMY

SECOND CORPS - MG John B. Gordon

Ramseur's Division - BG John Pegram (killed 2/6);
BG Robert D. Johnston

Pegram's Brigade - COL John S. Hoffman (wounded 2/5);
LT COL John G. Kasey
13th Virginia   31st Virginia   49th Virginia
52nd Virginia   58th Virginia

Lewis' Brigade - BG William G. Lewis
6th North Carolina   21st North Carolina
54th North Carolina   57th North Carolina

Johnston's Brigade - COL John W. Lea;
BG Gen. Robert D. Johnston
5th North Carolina   12th North Carolina
20th North Carolina   23rd North Carolina
1st North Carolina Battalion Sharpshooters

Gordon's Division - BG Clement A. Evans

Evans' Brigade - COL John H. Lowe
13th Georgia   26th Georgia   31st Georgia
38th Georgia   60th Georgia   61st Georgia
12th Georgia Artillery Battalion

Terry's Brigade - BG William Terry
2nd Virginia   4th Virginia   5th Virginia   10th Virginia
21st Virginia   23rd Virginia   25th Virginia   27th Virginia
33rd Virginia   37th Virginia   42nd Virginia
44th Virginia   48th Virginia

York's Brigade - COL William R. Peck
1st Louisiana   2nd Louisiana   5th Louisiana
6th Louisiana   7th Louisiana   8th Louisiana
9th Louisiana   10th Louisiana   14th Louisiana
15th Louisiana

Heth's Division - MG Henry Heth; BG Joseph R. Davis

Davis' Brigade - COL Andrew Mc. Nelson (captured);
COL Reuben O. Reynolds
2nd Mississippi   11th Mississippi
26th Mississippi   42nd Mississippi
1st Confederate Battalion

Cooke's Brigade - BG John R. Cooke
15th North Carolina   27th North Carolina
46th North Carolina   55th North Carolina

MacRae's Brigade - BG William MacRae
11th North Carolina   26th North Carolina
44th North Carolina   47th North Carolina
52nd North Carolina

McComb's Brigade - BG William McComb
1st Tennessee PA   7th Tennessee
14th Tennessee   17th Tennessee
23rd Tennessee   25th Tennessee
44th Tennessee   63rd Tennessee
2nd Maryland Battalion

Mahone's Division - BG Joseph Finegan

Weisiger's Brigade - BG David A. Weisiger
6th Virginia   12th Virginia   16th Virginia
41st Virginia   61st Virginia

Harris' Brigade - BG Nathaniel H. Harris
12th Mississippi   16th Mississippi
19th Mississippi   48th Mississippi

Sorrel's Brigade - BG Moxley Sorrel (wounded);
COL George E. Tayloe
3rd Georgia   22nd Georgia   48th Georgia
64th Georgia   2nd Georgia Battalion
10th Georgia Battalion

Finegan's Brigade - COL David Lang
2nd Florida   5th Florida   8th Florida
9th Florida   10th Florida   11th Florida
Bonaud's (Georgia) Battalion

Forney's Brigade - COL William H. Forney
8th Alabama   9th Alabama   10th Alabama
11th Alabama   13th Alabama   14th Alabama

Wilcox's Division - MG Cadmus M. Wilcox

McGowan's Brigade - BG Samuel McGowan
1st South Carolina PA   1st South Carolina Rifles
12th South Carolina   13th South Carolina
14th South Carolina

Scales' Brigade - COL Joseph H. Hyman
13th North Carolina   16th North Carolina
22nd North Carolina   34th North Carolina
38th North Carolina

CAVALRY

W. H. F. Lee's Division - William H. F. "Rooney" Lee
Barringer's Brigade - BG Rufus Barringer
1st North Carolina   2nd North Carolina
3rd North Carolina   5th North Carolina
Beale's Brigade - BG Richard L. T. Beale
9th Virginia   10th Virginia   13th Virginia

Dearing's Brigade - BG James Dearing
8th Georgia   4th North Carolina
16th North Carolina Battalion

ARTILLERY

Chew's Artillery Battalion
Virginia (McGregor's) Battery

Pegram's Artillery Battalion
Virginia (Ellett's) Battery

MAJ - Major; LT COL - Lt. Colonel; COL - Colonel;
BG - Brigadier General; MG - Major General.
Bvt. - brevet rank

Compiled by Chris Calkins

APPENDIX 2 — ORDER OF BATTLE

FIVE FORKS, April 1, 1865

UNION FORCES - MG Philip H. Sheridan

V CORPS, Army of the Potomac - MG Gouverneur K. Warren (relieved); BG Charles Griffin

Headquarters Escort, 4th Pennsylvania Cavalry, Co. C
Provost Guard, 104th New York

First Division - Bvt. MG Charles Griffin; Bvt. MG Joseph J. Bartlett

First Brigade - BG Joshua L. Chamberlain
185th New York   198th Pennsylvania

Second Brigade - Bvt. BG Edgar M. Gregory
187th New York   188th New York   189th New York

Third Brigade - Bvt. MG Joseph J. Bartlett; Bvt. BG Alfred L. Pearson

1st Maine Sharpshooters   20th Maine   32nd Massachusetts
1st Michigan   16th Michigan   83rd Pennsylvania
91st Pennsylvania   118th Pennsylvania   155th Pennsylvania

Second Division - Bvt. MG Romeyn B. Ayres

First Brigade - Bvt. BG Frederic Winthrop (mortally wounded);
COL James Grindlay; BG Joseph Hayes
5th New York   140th New York   146th New York
15th New York Heavy Artillery

Second Brigade - Bvt. BG Andrew W. Denison (wounded 3/31);
COL Richard N. Bowerman (wounded 4/1); COL David L. Stanton
1st Maryland   4th Maryland   7th Maryland   8th Maryland

Third Brigade - Bvt. BG James Gwyn
3rd Delaware   4th Delaware   8th Delaware (three cos.)
157th Pennsylvania (four cos.)   190th Pennsylvania
191st Pennsylvania   210th Pennsylvania

Third Division - Bvt. MG Samuel W. Crawford

First Brigade - COL John A. Kellogg
91st New York   6th Wisconsin   7th Wisconsin

Second Brigade - BG Henry Baxter
16th Maine   39th Massachusetts   97th New York
11th Pennsylvania   107th Pennsylvania

Third Brigade - Bvt. BG Richard Coulter
94th New York   95th New York   147th New York
56th Pennsylvania   88th Pennsylvania   121st Pennsylvania
142nd Pennsylvania

Unattached
1st Battalion, New York Sharpshooters

Artillery Brigade - Bvt. BG Charles S. Wainwright
1st New York Light, Batteries B, D & H
15th New York Heavy Artillery, Co. M
4th U.S., Battery B   5th U.S., Batteries D & G

CAVALRY - MG Philip H. Sheridan

Army of the Shenandoah - Bvt. MG Wesley Merritt
(effectively a Cavalry Corps)

First Division - BG Thomas C. Devin

First Brigade - COL Peter Stagg
1st Michigan   5th Michigan   6th Michigan   7th Michigan

Second Brigade - COL Charles L. Fitzhugh
6th New York   9th New York   19th New York (1st Dragoons)
17th Pennsylvania   20th Pennsylvania

Third (Reserve) Brigade - BG Alfred Gibbs
2nd Massachusetts   6th Pennsylvania (six cos.)
1st U.S.   5th U.S.   6th U.S.

Artillery
4th U.S., Batteries C & F

Third Division - Bvt. MG George A. Custer

First Brigade - COL Alexander C.M. Pennington
1st Connecticut   3rd New Jersey   2nd New York   2nd Ohio

Second Brigade - COL William Wells
8th New York   15th New York   1st Vermont

Third Brigade - COL Henry Capehart
1st New York (Lincoln)   1st West Virginia
2nd West Virginia (seven cos.)   3rd West Virginia

Second Division, Army of the Potomac - MG George Crook

First Brigade - BG Henry E. Davies, Jr.
1st New Jersey   10th New York   24th New York
1st Pennsylvania (five cos.)   2nd U.S., Battery A

Second Brigade - Bvt. BG J. Irvin Gregg;
COL Samuel B.M. Young
4th Pennsylvania   8th Pennsylvania (eight cos.)
16th Pennsylvania   21st Pennsylvania
1st U.S., Batteries H & I

Third Brigade - Bvt. BG Charles H. Smith
1st Maine   2nd New York Mtd. Rifles   6th Ohio   13th Ohio

Cavalry Division - BG Ranald S. Mackenzie

First Brigade - COL Robert M. West
20th New York, Co. G   5th Pennsylvania

Second Brigade - COL Samuel P. Spear
1st District of Columbia (battalion)   1st Maryland
11th Pennsylvania

Artillery
4th Wisconsin Light

CONFEDERATE FORCES

FIRST CORPS, Army of Northern Virginia - LG James Longstreet

Pickett's Division - MG George E. Pickett

Steuart's Brigade - BG George H. Steuart
9th Virginia   14th Virginia   38th Virginia
53rd Virginia   57th Virginia

Corse's Brigade - BG Montgomery Corse; COL Arthur Herbert
15th Virginia   17th Virginia   29th Virginia
30th Virginia   32nd Virginia

Hunton's Brigade - BG Eppa Hunton; MAJ Michael P. Spessard
8th Virginia   18th Virginia   19th Virginia
28th Virginia   56th Virginia

Terry's Brigade - BG William R. Terry; MAJ William W. Bentley
1st Virginia   3rd Virginia   7th Virginia
11th Virginia   24th Virginia

ANDERSON'S CORPS - LG Richard H. Anderson

Johnson's Division - MG Bushrod R. Johnson;
BG William H. Wallace

Wise's Brigade - BG Henry A. Wise
26th Virginia   34th Virginia   46th Virginia   59th Virginia

Wallace's Brigade - BG William H. Wallace
17th South Carolina   18th South Carolina
22nd South Carolina   23rd South Carolina
26th South Carolina
Holcombe Legion Infantry Battalion

Moody's Brigade - BG Young M. Moody
41st Alabama   43rd Alabama   59th Alabama
60th Alabama   23rd Alabama Battalion

Ransom's Brigade - BG Matthew W. Ransom
24th North Carolina   25th North Carolina
35th North Carolina   49th North Carolina
56th North Carolina

Artillery

Pegram's Battalion - COL William J. Pegram;
LT COL Joseph McGraw

Heth's Division - MG Henry Heth; BG Joseph R. Davis

Cooke's Brigade - BG John R. Cooke
15th North Carolina   27th North Carolina
46th North Carolina   48th North Carolina
55th North Carolina

MacRae's Brigade - BG William MacRae
11th North Carolina   26th North Carolina
44th North Carolina   47th North Carolina
52nd North Carolina

CAVALRY CORPS, Army of Northern Virginia - MG Fitzhugh Lee

Fitzhugh Lee's Division - COL Thomas T. Munford

Payne's Brigade - BG William H. Payne; COL Reuben B. Boston
5th Virginia   6th Virginia   8th Virginia
36th Virginia Battalion

Munford's Brigade
1st Virginia   2nd Virginia   3rd Virginia   4th Virginia

William H.F. Lee's Division - MG William H.F. Lee

Barringer's Brigade - BG Rufus Barringer

1st North Carolina   2nd North Carolina
3rd North Carolina   5th North Carolina

Beale's Brigade - CPT Samuel H. Burt
9th Virginia   10th Virginia   13th Virginia   14th Virginia

Roberts' Brigade - BG William P. Roberts
4th North Carolina   16th North Carolina Battalion

Rosser's Division - MG Thomas L. Rosser

Dearing's Brigade - BG James Dearing
7th Virginia   11th Virginia   12th Virginia   35th Virginia Battalion

McCausland's Brigade
16th Virginia   17th Virginia   21st Virginia   22nd Virginia

Artillery
Chew's Battalion

McGregor's Battery (Graham's and Brown's)
CPT William M. McGregor

CPT - Captain; MAJ - Major; LT COL - Lt. Colonel;
COL - Colonel; BG - Brigadier General; MG - Major General,
LG - Lieutenant General. Bvt. - brevet rank

Compiled by Chris Calkins

APPENDIX 3

So, What Are Shad?

And How Did They Affect Confederate Fortunes at Five Forks?

by Dave Roth
Editor, *Blue & Gray Magazine*

Shad, known to zoologists as *Alosa sapidissima*, are members of the herring family that can be found along both American coasts, though at the time of the Civil War the fish was predominantly an Atlantic catch. A shad is blue or blue-green on its back and upper parts with a silvery color below, can weigh as much as 14 pounds, and reaches 30 inches in length. It dines on insects and insect larvae, small fish and crustaceans, and sometimes tiny plant life. Primarily marine creatures, shad ascend far up coastal rivers during late winter and early spring to spawn. They have very delicate and toothless mouths and are generally caught with nets, though shad can put up a good fight on light tackle. (George Washington once ran a shad operation, using a seine, on the Potomac River.) Dusk and dawn are the best catch times. Shad generally do not feed on the upriver run but will strike at certain lures, such as small shiny darts with a bit of a tail. The inland run on most rivers is now restricted by the presence of dams. The major annoyance in dining on shad is avoiding the multitude of tiny bones. Baking the fish in a covered roaster at 250 degrees for about eight hours causes the bones to disintegrate. According to Tidewater Virginians, shad is exquisite when served with bourbon or brandy.

The foregoing description of the fish that affected Confederate fortunes at Five Forks is hardly controversial. But the following letters among the unpublished personal papers of Thomas T. Munford led him to conclude that George Pickett was full of shad and more on April 1, 1865:

I think you are mistaken in the opinion that the Battle of Five Forks is not generally understood by the survivors of the Army of Northern Virginia. The shad lunch, the whiskey, and the sad catastrophe to the Army of Northern Virginia, of which they were the prime factors—were well known & deplored at the time & they are remembered today with keen regret. I wish they could be obliterated from our Confederate annals. Five Forks is the chief blot upon the otherwise fair and glorious record of Gen. Lee's army. — Robert W. Hunter, former staff officer to General John B. Gordon, CSA, to Thomas T. Munford, October 19, 1904

Pickett joined me about 2 o'clock [April 1, 1865]. We lunched together on some fine shad which [General James] Dearing and I had caught in the Nott[o]way two days before. While with me my pickets reported the enemy advancing on all the roads bearing [on] . . . Five Forks which fact I communicated to Gen'l Pickett, but being present he examined the courier himself as to the facts reported. An hour or two passed and report after report was received as to the approach of the enemy when finally Gen'l Pickett ordered me to send a trooper with a message from him to Gen'l Matt Ransom (I think) at Five Forks. . . . Fitz Lee came . . . with Pickett and lunched with us. . . . — Thomas L. Rosser to James Longstreet, October 22, 1892

I found Genl Fitz Lee & Pickett sitting under a fly tent — at least 2 miles in your [Munford's] rear, with a bottle of whiskey or Brandy, I don't know which for I was not invited to partake of it. I delivered your message & he told me to tell you to do the best you could. I remember full well that you looked much disappointed at the order I brought you. . . . — J. B. Flippin, formerly a sergeant in the 3rd Virginia Cavalry, to Thomas T. Munford, undated

. . . it was hardly exaggerated when you speak of that fatal lunch as the ruin of the Confederacy. It certainly did at least hasten the catastrophe. — Former Confederate President Jefferson Davis, written May 28, 1889, from his home "Beauvoir" in Mississippi, to Thomas T. Munford

INDEX

INDEX

Numbers in **bold** indicate a photograph.

The General's Books is an Affiliate of Blue & Gray Magazine

Blue & Gray Magazine, founded in 1983, is a bi-monthly, 68-pg., full-color periodical devoted to a travel approach to the Civil War. The magazine is proud to publish such fine authors as Ted Alexander, Stacy Allen, Ed Bearss, Chris Calkins, Albert Castel, Gary Gallagher, A. Wilson Greene, Robert K. and Robert E. L. Krick, William Marvel, Richard McMurry, Wiley Sword, Terry Winschel, and many others. To subscribe to the magazine, write to 522 Norton Rd., Columbus, OH 43228, or call toll-free **1-800-CIVIL WAR** (800-248-4592). Website: www.bluegraymagazine.com. One-year (6 issues) $19.95; two-year $36.95; three-year $48.95. Check, money order, Visa, MasterCard and American Express accepted. Write for a list of back issues. If you wish to order any of the books listed below, you can call **1-800-CIVIL WAR** and use your credit card, or send a check or money order to the street address above. For shipping & handling include $6.00 for the first book, $1.50 each additional book. Ohio residents must include 5.75% sales tax.

Titles from The General's Books

Embrace An Angry Wind, The Confederacy's Last Hurrah: Spring Hill, Franklin and Nashville *by Wiley Sword. 528 pp., hardcover, dust jacket*..$34.95

William Clarke Quantrill: His Life and Times *by Albert Castel. 256 pp., hardcover, dust jacket. Illustrated. Index*......................................$24.95

Yankee Quaker Confederate General: The Curious Career of Bushrod Rust Johnson *by Charles M. Cummings. 435 pp., hardcover, dust jacket. Illustrated. Index. New Endnote by Noble K. Wyatt, who moved Johnson's body from an obscure cemetery in Illinois to his wife's side in a Nashville cemetery*......................................$24.95

The Fifteenth Ohio Volunteer Infantry and Its Campaigns 1861-1865 *by Captain Alexis Cope, Regimental and Brigade Adjutant. 872 pp., hardcover, dust jacket. Illustrated. Roster and Index added. One of Fox's "Fighting 300" Regiments*......................$45.00

The Story of Camp Chase: A History of the Prison and Its Cemetery . . . *by William H. Knauss. 424 pp., hardcover, dust jacket. Illustrated. Index. Memorial Edition with photos added*......................................$29.95

General Wesley Merritt: Brandy Station to Manila Bay *by Don E. Alberts, PhD. 372 pp., hardcover, dust jacket. Revised edition. Illustrated. New index*......................................$31.95

Tour Guides and Visitors Guides from Blue & Gray Magazine

Blue & Gray Magazine's History and Tour Guide of the Antietam Battlefield *by the Editors of Blue & Gray Magazine with Stephen W. Sears and James V. Murfin. 160 pp., softcover. Illustrated. 17 maps. Order of Battle. Index*......................................$9.95

Blue & Gray Magazine's Guide to Haunted Places of the Civil War *176 pp., softcover. 83 illustrations. Features 19 haunted sites*......................................$12.95

Shiloh—A Visitors Guide *by Stacy D. Allen, Shiloh park historian. Full-color, 76 pp., 15 maps, 8.5 x 11 softcover*......................$8.95

Forgotten Valor: Off the Beaten Path at Antietam—A Visitors Guide *by Ted Alexander, Antietam park historian. Full-color, 28 pp., 3 maps, 8.5 x 11 softcover*......................$3.95

The Battle of Averasboro, North Carolina, March 15-16, 1865—A Visitors Guide *by Mark L. Bradley. Full-color, 28 pp., 4 maps, 8.5 x 11 softcover*......................................$3.95

Books Distributed for Genesis Publishing

Reminiscences of General Basil W. Duke *by Duke. 626 pp., hardcover, dust jacket*......................$39.95

Wild Riders of the First Kentucky Cavalry (US)—"Wolford's Cavalry" *by Eastham Tarrant. 632 pp., hardcover, dust jacket*......................................$39.95